Fixing Government Flaws

Amending Our Constitution to Save Our Representative Democracy

Dale Leitzke

ISBN: 979-8-218-38290-2 (paperback)

Fixing Government Flaws: Amending Our Constitution to Save Our Representative Democracy is a game changer. It describes a step-by-step procedure from public sentiment to ratification. Instead of ruminating about details of Constitutional law, it discusses real world methods of using available tools and our Founder's examples to amend the Constitution. Article V of the Constitution provides an opportunity to make changes to campaign financing, redistricting, health care, gun laws, and ensure fair elections. The book is powerful in its defense of the people's right to correct our government's flaws, using the words of the Constitution and interests of the voters to avoid oligarchy and autocracy.

Table of Contents

Introduction

In 1964 Bob Dylan wrote *"he not busy being born, is busy dying."* This poet laureate was speaking of the human emotional experience, but the sentiment can apply to government. Governments continue to reinvent themselves or eventually lose their power.

The forces that guide that reinvention are critical to the success of a representative democracy. When we choose deliberate reasoning as a guiding force, long-term government success is likely. But choosing passion as the driving force weakens our system of government, and its long-term success is problematic. Our Founders understood this.

Passion and deliberate reasoning are competing forces. Positive feelings toward government create time and opportunity for deliberate reasoning. Anti-government sentiment invokes passion. Today's highly partisan atmosphere magnifies these competing forces.

It is helpful to see where we have been and where we are going. In the first generations after we won the Revolutionary War, we were busy being born. We adopted the Constitution, added territory, and passed amendments to the Constitution. We also faced and repelled a foreign threat. Positive emotions were high.

Although deliberate reasoning guided our Founders when they drafted the Constitution, it could not overcome the original sin of slavery. The Founders reasoned that keeping the thirteen states together would be better militarily and economically than other options. In the generations prior to the Civil War, we added territory and successfully faced foreign challenges. The slavery issue influenced our feelings about the government. No new constitutional amendments were added in the fifty-seven years prior to the Civil War.

We fought the Civil War over slavery and its economic impact. But neither side directed their passions against the concept of a representative democracy. Today's partisan divide displays passion that may be even more dangerous.

For the next hundred years we added territory and fought off foreign threats. We added Constitutional amendments. Congress passed major legislation to curb monopolies and create a social safety net. Winning foreign wars contributed to positive feelings toward government.

Unrest in the 1960's brought out anger and passion. Street protests were common as we exercised our First Amendment rights. Young people used youthful exuberance to shake the windows and rattle the walls. Senators and members of Congress heeded the call, and the country grew stronger. Desire for a change in government was the driving force. As a result, Congress passed major civil rights legislation, and voted for new amendments to the Constitution. Our government was reinventing itself. One might say that our government was still busy being born.

A generation later, forces affecting our attitude toward government began to change. The Cold War threat faded. We stopped adding new amendments to the Constitution and stopped reinventing ourselves. That trend has continued. History shows that many governments failed because they did not adapt to evolving threats and changing demands of new generations.

A contributing factor in the fall of Ancient Greece was the lower classes revolting against the upper classes and ruling elites. Plato believed that those favoring autocracy exploited free speech to install themselves as tyrants.

The fall of the Roman Empire had many contributing factors including urban decay, failure to unite diverse cultures, an often-violent transfer of power, and political corruption. When expansion of the empire stopped, the decline started.

Recent history has seen fascism reject reason in the name of will, often denying truth in favor of a sinister ideology. Communist rulers used a well-organized political party that claimed to have the world's best knowledge of reason and government function. These regimes took over when prior democracies could not adapt quickly enough to prevent autocratic rule.

Our grand experiment in democracy has survived due to its ability to react to public sentiment while avoiding the ever-present pitfalls that toppled other ancient and modern governments. As public sentiment changes and our government does not react, we risk being just another chapter in a history book. Our democratic heritage, contrary to substantial public opinion, does not protect us from this fate. James Madison and the rest of our Founders set the table for success, but they could not predict ongoing changes and therefore could not ensure the long-term success of the government that they created. That is up to the politically divided nation that we have today.

The generation of the 1960's and 1970's faced a different political and governmental environment. The gap between the rich and poor was far narrower. Lower income Americans had less reason to distrust government and corporations. Media outlets showed only limited political bias. Health care costs were not a major concern. Climate change was not on anyone's radar screen. Both political parties included members with moderate ideologies and politicians were willing to compromise. Our government reacted to the will of its people.

In the 2000 election, political bias caused the Secretary of State in the State of Florida to stop the recount of votes for President. That biased act caused the Republican candidate to become

President of the United States. The transfer of power was peaceful, but the wound caused by the political bias remains. That act resulted in Republican nominated Supreme Court justices and continued Republican domination of the court.

In 2008, the Supreme Court decided 5-4 that citizens have the right to bear arms for personal defense. Firearms sales and gun related deaths have increased dramatically since then. Gun deaths are now the number one killer of our children.

In 2010, the Supreme Court ruled 5-4 that limiting the free speech of corporations and other groups violated the First Amendment, allowing them to spend unlimited sums of money on political campaigns. Prior to this ruling, the United Nations had equated this dark money to corruption. Spending on elections in this country has doubled since that Supreme Court ruling.

In 2016, the Republican Party refused to have confirmation hearings on a Supreme Court nominee thus stealing a seat on the United States Supreme Court from Democrats.

Changes in government structure and function that occurred since the 1960's and 1970's are cause for concern. The way that we have faced ongoing challenges has slowly changed. Our government has evolved into one that is less responsive to the concerns of its citizens. Some of the most notable concerns are discussed here.

Election Related Issues

Citizens United v FEC

On January 21, 2010, this Supreme Court decision overruled the *Austin vs. Michigan Chamber of Commerce* decision made twenty years earlier. In his minority opinion, Justice Stevens and the dissent predicted the rise in money infiltrating politics with an ominous quote, *"A democracy cannot function effectively when its constituent members believe laws are being bought and sold."* The Brennan Center for Justice represents itself as a nonpartisan law and policy institute. It made the following comments on *Citizens United.*

"The 2010 decision further tilted political influence toward wealthy donors and corporations. That decision reversed century-old campaign finance restrictions and enabled corporations and other outside groups to spend unlimited funds on elections with negative repercussions for American democracy and the fight against political corruption. In recent polls, 94 percent of Americans blamed wealthy political donors for political dysfunction. The most significant outcomes of Citizens United have been the creation of super PACs, which empower the

wealthiest donors, and the expansion of dark money through shadowy nonprofits that do not publicly report their donors. In the 2018 election cycle, for example, the top 100 donors to super PACs contributed nearly 78 percent of all super PAC spending."

Dark money expenditures increased from around five million in 2006 to 300 million in 2012. The Conversation Report said that a record eleven billion was spent on campaigns in 2020, mostly from a handful of super-rich donors.

Previously, the court had upheld certain spending restrictions, arguing that the government had a role in preventing corruption. But in *Citizens United*, a bare majority of the justices held that *"independent political spending"* did not present a substantive threat of corruption.

Super PACs (Political Action Committees) must show their donors, but those donors can include dark money groups, which makes the original source of the donations unclear. It is difficult to determine if funding comes from foreign sources. We simply do not know if large sums of money are coming in from our foreign adversaries to elect candidates or promote causes that favor the interest of those foreign adversaries.

Other developed countries, like Canada and the United Kingdom, impose stricter spending limits on political campaigns.

A 2018 poll by the Center for Public Integrity found that three fourths of Americans back a constitutional amendment outlawing *Citizens United*.

That included sixty-six percent of Republicans and eighty-five percent of Democrats. Abraham Lincoln warned in his first inaugural address that *"if the policy of the Government upon vital questions affecting the whole people is to be irrevocably fixed by decisions of the Supreme Court, then the people will have ceased to be their own rulers."*

With the *Citizens* ruling, the court has effectively created law. The decision to allow corporations to exercise freedom of speech with campaign donations has made constitutional precedent. Congress had passed campaign finance laws in the previous years. The non-delegation doctrine offers guidance that tells us that the court has no business making laws. That opportunity belongs solely to Congress per Article I of the Constitution. Any authoritarian ruler would be proud of this ruling because it shows power from the top and not power of public opinion.

If ninety four percent of Americans blame wealthy donors for political dysfunction, the *Citizens* ruling can be a contributing factor in anti-government sentiment. Republicans blame wealthy Democratic donors and Democrats blame wealthy Republican donors. Anti-government sentiment favors those who market distrust of government with the objective of replacing our representative democracy with a more autocrat regime.

Traditionally, the Republican Party has voted with corporate interests. But the interest of larger corporations is not a true representation of the interest of all Republicans and certainly not the interest of all Americans. The Supreme Court became its own echo chamber of political thinking as it built momentum with consecutive rulings favoring corporations. This occurred over recent years and was the work of judges appointed by Republican presidents. These Republican appointees have dominated the court for several decades. Cynically, these judges have turned the Lincoln quote *"government of the people, by the people, and for the people."* to government of the people, by the politicians, and for the wealthy, the special interest groups, and the corporations.

It is the wealthy and their collaborators. Collaborators include leaders of major corporate interests such as the fossil fuel industry, pharmaceutical, insurance, banking, gun manufacturers, the religious right, and right-wing extremist organizations. These groups do not have preservation of representative democracy as a top priority. Greed and lust for power drive their actions.

Too many of our elected representatives are heavily influenced by those that supply financial support. They have each become puppets on a string with the biggest donors pulling the strings. The *Citizens United* ruling has indirectly caused some elected representatives to align themselves with corruption and autocracy.

A new amendment to the Constitution could overturn this ruling.

Gerrymandering

We may define gerrymandering as the manipulation of an electoral constituency's boundaries for the purpose of favoring one party or class. Some pundits say that gerrymandering protects the party lines and keeps bad incumbents in power.

In simple terms, it is legalized election cheating. Wayne Dawkins described gerrymandering as politicians picking their voters instead of voters picking their politicians. The process throws shade on the concept of free and fair elections. This is one of the reasons that our rating is below a *"full democracy"* on the Democracy Index (set up by a well-recognized British economist group). The United States Supreme Court, the one institution that could enforce proper checks and balances on this issue, has chosen to punt the issue back the states. The *Rucho* decision carried water for the wealthy and their collaborators. It ensures that red states and blue states will continue the practice of partisan gerrymandering.

The Brennan Center for Justice said that Republicans had a net gain of sixteen to seventeen Congressional seats in the last decade due to gerrymandering. Free and fair elections, with no gerrymandering, would have given Democrats control of the United States House of Representatives today's 117th Congress, not Republicans. Freedom House pointed to gerrymandering and other barriers to voting as *"the most corrosive and radicalizing effect on U.S. politics."* Justice John Paul Stevens wrote that *"ending political gerrymandering will help to promote political compromise."*

A 2017 bipartisan poll conducted by Democratic researcher Celinda Lake and Republican analyst Ashlee Rich Stephenson found that seventy-one percent of Americans would like the Supreme Court to define a standard that ends partisan gerrymandering. This cuts across party lines: eighty percent of Democrats, sixty-eight percent of independents, and sixty-five percent of Republicans would back that action by the Court.

The history of gerrymandering in this country began long before we had computers. But with computers the practice became enhanced. And since we have not recently corrected any constitutional flaws, the practice has gone mostly unchecked.

A United States House of Representatives, influenced by gerrymandering, passed laws that favored the rich and corporations and passed laws on social hot button issues such as abortion, gay rights, voting rights, and union rights. Overall, the Republican Party more often uses gerrymandering. The result of this legalized cheating favors its ideology.

It begs credulity to believe the *Rucho* decision would have been the same if gerrymandering favored the Democratic Party instead of the Republican Party. Implying that the ruling represented proper jurisprudence is blatant hypocrisy. Rather than fairness we get the same old song from politicians and the courts; do not change the rules because they help me to defeat my opposition.

Our allowed level of gerrymandering is unique among other democratic nations. In other nations, this legalized election cheating is not a significant factor. Amplification of this process increases our widening partisan divide.

We could ban gerrymandering with an amendment to the Constitution.

Electing the President

Our system of electing the President does not instill a high degree of confidence in the American people. The Electoral College, leftover from our early history, is vulnerable to unscrupulous actors. Other countries have a higher level of confidence when electing their leaders.

According to a 2020 Gallup poll, sixty-one percent of Americans support abolishing the Electoral College.

From the perspective of Presidential elections, we are the 'united states' of America and not the united people of America. The states elect the President, not the people. But in recent elections we have faced two potential problems. Population demographics now dictate that Democrats must win about fifty-one and a half percent of the vote to elect a Democratic President. This contributed to the fact that in two recent elections, the Republican candidate received fewer votes than the Democrat but won the Presidency.

Another potential problem is related to gerrymandering. Republicans have gerrymandered more representatives in the House of Representatives. If neither candidate receives a majority of Electoral College votes, each state's Congressional delegation casts one vote for President, determining the winner. That gives Wyoming the same number of votes as California. This tie breaker favors Republicans because there are more red states than blue states.

Sinister Republican actors understand that disruption of the certification of votes in the Electoral College automatically gives the election to the Republican candidate. That is a major incentive to interfere with the state's certification of its votes. By claiming election fraud and not allowing a state to cast its electoral votes, the total electoral votes may come up short for both candidates. That may throw the election into the United States House of Representatives and guarantee a Republican victory.

In the 2000 election, the Florida Republican secretary of state, without a specific objective reason, stopped the recount. We may remember the 'hanging chads' controversy. As a result, the election resulted in victory for George W. Bush rather than Al Gore. A similar action, not supported by an objective reason, conducted by a Republican secretary of state could flip a future presidential election.

Our Founders did not see this opening for unscrupulous actors. It reduces confidence in our election process and our government.

One solution to the perceived problem is to elect the President based on the popular vote. A 2022 Pew Research poll showed that sixty-three percent of Americans prefer a popular vote for President over the current Electoral College system. Many other developed countries do this. But conservatives will argue that this would be changing existing constitutional rules. Other developed countries have smaller populations. A national recount in a close election could be cumbersome and could cause a constitutional crisis in an election with a razor thin victory margin.

The current rule is that the states, because of states' rights, cast the votes. If we change the rules to a popular vote, small states could object and say that they would be losing power. It is true that they now have more electoral power than they would in a direct vote election. The Constitution may guarantee that electoral power as part of the equal suffrage provision of Article V.

An alternative compromise solution may reduce the incentive for bad actors and not reduce voting power of the small states. Currently each state, whether it is California with a large population or Wyoming with a small population, gets two extra electoral votes along with its population-allocated-state votes. That small states' advantage would remain.

This alternative solution relies on fair redistricting in every state. Maine and Nebraska have electoral votes distributed by congressional districts. The Presidential candidate with the most popular vote in each congressional district gets one electoral vote. The candidate that wins the most popular votes for that state wins two additional electoral votes.

That would be fair for all fifty states if redistricting is fair. The total number of electoral votes would remain the same as it is today. This would decrease the accidental unfair distribution of electoral votes and reduce the probability of electing a 'minority President.' The accidental unfairness has only occurred in the last thirty years. But it is a flaw in our Constitution that we may correct.

This new system would effectively end the concept of swing states. Candidates would develop a national campaign, not just a swing states campaign.

The second part of this alternative solution involves a change in the tie-breaker rules. Instead of sending the election into the United States House of Representatives, if no candidate wins the most electoral votes, the candidate with the most popular vote wins the election. This tiebreaker may occur if a third-party candidate received enough electoral votes to prevent one candidate from getting a majority. It also deters nefarious players from disrupting the certification of their state's electoral vote. This was not an issue during our first two hundred years, but an increasing partisan divide and recent close elections have highlighted this constitutional flaw that encourages bad actors.

An amendment to the Constitution is necessary to change our system of electing a President.

Term Limits on Congress

Many of us would like to get rid of members of the United States Congress that we do not like. Term limits sound good. But major change is scary. We need experienced legislators. This is especially true in the United States Senate where they discuss major foreign policy issues. And the Speaker of the United States House of Representatives should have enough experience to lead competently.

According to a group called United States Term Limits, eighty-two percent of citizens want term limits for members of Congress. Polls can be deceiving. Everyone wants better government but are the polls just expressing a general dissatisfaction or are they expressing support for a system that has a proven history? The polls may be like a Christmas wish list.

If the polls are wrong, then let the votes of the people give us better national information. Debates prior to voting clarify specific issues. Polling may only reflect vague general sentiment. Robust debates are critical. Polls are not.

We do not need members of Congress who are older and less productive than those typically found in competing private organization jobs like corporate CEO's. We should not have members of Congress who win reelection only by name recognition, enhanced incumbent fund-raising ability, or entrenched, often graft-like, political connections.

We may consider two competing approaches here. The first is more pragmatic and considers historical precedent as well as the need to weed out aging weak members of Congress. The second considers polling data and the national desire to reduce the number of entrenched members of Congress in hopes that this will reduce political corruption.

Currently, some members of Congress stay in office for thirty years or more. Age limits may be unconstitutional. The average number of years of service for members of the House is about ten years and for the Senate it is now about thirteen years.

The Senate may be a more important body when it comes to checks and balances on government action. We should not overcorrect the problem. The best and the brightest should have an opportunity to stay longer. A normalized tenure pattern may be that the longest tenure is double that of the average tenure. That would lead to term limits of twenty-four years for the Senate and twenty for the House.

But the recent rise in tenure in the House may be due to excessive party loyalty or an increase in campaign expenditure.

The average for the House may need a logical adjustment to account for the recent, unwarranted, increase in tenure. The 1955 to 1997 average tenure for the House was eight years. Double of that is sixteen years.

That is drastic for the House considering the uncapped tenures have occasionally lasted more than thirty years. Further reduction in term limits may reduce the competency of House leadership. One may question the competency of the Speaker of the House if their experience level is less than fourteen years. History shows that the House Speaker often had twenty-four or more years of experience. Term limits of sixteen years for the House and twenty-four years for the Senate may still seem like a long time to set up excessive party loyalties. But our leadership should not exclude long tenure of the best and the brightest. One factor that could also reduce congressional terms is Ranked Choice Voting (discussed below). A constitutional amendment should not exclude other ways to solve a perceived problem by using constitutional measures that are too drastic.

Using actual data, we can calculate the number of Congresspeople and Senators that would lose office each election cycle due to term limits. It is about twenty for the House and four for the Senate. Nineteen percent of members of the House of

Representatives now stay longer than sixteen years. Twelve percent of the Senators have been in office over twenty-four years.

A thought experiment is helpful here. If today's aging members of Congress were theoretically running for the same office, at the same age, but had no experience in Congress, would their age cause them to compete for office less effectively? If the answer is yes, then we can see that their reelection and extended term in office is primarily based on party loyalty, name recognition, and ability to bring-home-the-bacon for their constituents because of their seniority and power. Those aging members of Congress, lacking competitive competency, may help their constituents but harm the overall competency of their body of Congress.

These shorter-term limits will move the upper age of members of Congress limit more toward the upper age limit in competing private jobs, not beyond that limit. That is a win for the whole country. With the House having shorter term limits than the Senate, the average age of a House member will be lower than that of a Senator. That may be a good thing; youthful vigor on one hand and age and experience on the other hand.

Combined total service should also be logical. We may suggest thirty years. Small states are the concern. A member of the house in a small state has an easy path to the Senate. Sixteen years in the House plus twenty-four years in the Senate totals forty years. That is too long but at the same time we should not exclude a termed-out congressperson from running for the Senate. Thirty years is a reasonable compromise.

The second approach would lead to more drastic term limits.

The overall objective should be electing the best possible representatives; the best and brightest individuals who are least corrupt and most likely to serve the constituents instead of party interests, wealthy donors, or special interests.

Elections are every other year for members of the House. That means that members spend an enormous amount of time campaigning and fundraising for each election cycle instead of lawmaking or serving constituent's needs. It is like one year of lawmaking and one year of running for reelection. In addition to infusing new members into Congress, term limits would mandate a group that would spend less time running for office.

Those lame-duck members would be less threatened by party leaders who might otherwise reduce their position in the party or create a primary challenger in the next election if that person voted their conscience instead of the party line.

In 1975, Congressional staff size was frozen. Since that time, the number of constituents per member of Congress has increased by fifty-four per cent due to the overall increase in the population of the United States. Increasing the staffing for members of Congress or increasing the size of

Congress are both problematic while one party sees the government as being too large. Electing the most effective lawmakers is the best short-term solution.

Numerous studies show that ninety-one percent of members of Congress who run for reelection are successful. Both effective and ineffective lawmakers get reelected due to factors favoring the incumbent. Voters have only a limited opportunity to weed out ineffective legislators.

A six-year term limit for members of the House would have three positive advantages. First, in every third election the race would be much more likely to have a contested race, even in safe districts. Secondly, lame-duck members would not have to campaign for reelection.

The third positive advantage is that an increase in competitive races creates an increase in public awareness of the issues and increases voter turnout. An informed electorate was part of George Washington's recommendation in his Farewell Address. Senators read that address aloud in front of the United States Senate each year.

If one of those terms was for four years, the member would only shoulder the need to campaign in one of the three terms.

Along with six-year term limits for the House of Representatives, we may have twelve-year term limits for the Senate.

The most credible criticism of term limits is that rules would require that the best, brightest, and most experienced lawmakers would leave office. But it is not necessary that they leave the office forever. If the objective is to create competitive races and give the public an opportunity to weed out less-effective lawmakers, we can let those termed-out lawmakers run for office later, say four years after their original term expires. That would create scenarios where a former congressperson might run against an incumbent. Those races are likely to be highly competitive even in safe red or safe blue districts. The best and the brightest would have the opportunity to continue their service.

Former members of Congress often lobby for special interests. For conflict-of-interest reasons, it would be best if the law prohibited these former lobbyists from running for Congressional office again.

Either the first or second approach may be desirable. An open and robust debate will lead us to the best choice.

An amendment to the Constitution is not mandatory to invoke term limits on members of Congress. But it is foolhardy to think that these power brokers would voluntarily limit the term of their own power.

Ranked Choice Voting

Years ago, when voting patterns in congressional districts showed a moderately similar number of voters from each party, primary elections were just a warmup for a contested general election.

But we now have more congressional districts that are strongly Democratic or strongly Republican. We find evidence of the increasing polarization by examining a series of presidential elections. In 1960 the average margin of victory in the presidential election for individual states was eight percent. In recent presidential elections these margins of victory increased to seventeen percent and eighteen percent. In blue states and red states, the winner in the presidential election often has a margin of victory of thirty percent or more. In today's bright red or bright blue districts, the primary is the critical election. The primary election candidate must only win over voters in that party. To do that, the candidate must follow party-line ideology. And as our partisan divide widens, the party ideology drifts farther from centrist views. Today a centrist candidate, who allows for compromise and country over party, may lose in the primary election to highly partisan candidates. Therefore, the winning candidates have more radical views and do not necessarily put country over party.

The fact that primary elections typically have low voter turnout worsens the problem. While general elections bring out fifty-five percent to seventy percent of voters, primary elections often bring out only fifteen percent to thirty percent of the voters. Voters that do turn out are commonly closer to the extreme end of the political spectrum than those who vote in general elections. As a result, candidates campaigning in primary elections must satisfy only those ideologically extreme elements of their party. And when primary candidates happen to be in safe districts where the primary victor is almost certain to win the general election, extremist candidates end up in state legislatures or the United States Congress.

According to Arnold Ventures, a philanthropic group, only fifty-nine out of 435 races for the United States House of Representatives were competitive in 2020. Cynically, that means that eighty-six percent of American voters knew who was going to win the congressional district race before they voted. We should not expect voters to do their homework and engage in civics discussions when the outcome has already by decided.

The issue of non-competitive races has developed in recent decades. If we wish to have more members of Congress that put country over party, we need to elect member of Congress with a more centrist ideology. Centrist legislators are more likely to compromise and address flaws in our government.

Ranked choice voting (RCV) points us in that direction. This system has an open primary. A voter does not need to be a member of either party to cast a vote. Moderate and independent voters are disenfranchised when they are shut out of primary elections. These are the voters that would choose candidates that could narrow the partisan gap. They are stuck with ideologically extreme candidate choices in November. Over twenty-six million voters do not participate in primary elections because they have not declared their party intentions. This occurs because half of the states have closed primaries.

With RCV, also called instant runoff voting or final five, all Republican and all Democratic primary candidates compete on the same ballot. The top four or five candidates win the opportunity to have their names on the general election ballots. In that election, the ranked-choice system allows voters to pick a second, third, and fourth choice for that office.

Voters can also do what they always have done, for example, just vote for their preferred candidate. Or they can rank their choices. If no candidate gets over fifty percent of the first-choice ballots, this system drops the lowest-ranked candidate, and adds the second choices of the voters to the higher-ranked candidates. This process continues until a candidate gets over fifty percent and wins the election.

In purple districts where Democrats and Republican always end up in a competitive race, the election results may not change because candidates with highly partisan views tend to lose the general election to the other political party. But in safe districts where the primary has been the deciding election, the dynamic will change some of the outcomes. Candidates with a more centrist ideology may survive the primary election. All candidates would need to seek support from the general election voters and not merely the more partisan primary voters. In 'safe' districts it would be more likely that a second Republican or a second Democrat would be on the ballot in the general election.

The best and the brightest among more centrist potential candidates may realize that a radical incumbent might beat them in a closed primary, but with RCV the more centrist candidate may still win the general election. This may cause the more centrist candidates to run for office.

As of 2022, two states have implemented RCV for federal elections, Maine, and Alaska. An Additional sixteen states have or are planning some degree of RCV application. Oregon and Nevada will have the issue on the ballot in 2024.

Maine used RCV in 2018 and 2020 and election turnout was higher. Several studies in large cities that used RCV showed increased turnout in primary and general elections. Two of the studies showed a ten percent turnout increase. None of the studies showed a turnout decline. Logically, voters are more interested in a contested race. When turnout is high, winners are more likely to reflect the will of the entire voting public.

Historical data shows that a higher voter turnout favors Democrats. It is therefore not surprising to see Republican opposition to RCV. Effective voter suppression wins elections for Republicans. It is worthy of note that if we extrapolate voter suppression to the nth degree, we have autocracy.

RCV can cause delays in the reporting of the election results. This happens when no candidate receives more than fifty percent of the first-round vote. A one-to-two-week delay is possible. In these contests, RCV replaces the possibility of a runoff election. It is a matter of choice and fairness. Georgia has chosen runoff elections. Runoffs are expensive.

Ranked-choice voting will also cause candidates to tone down some of the scorched-earth rhetoric thrown at their opponents because they will seek to be chosen as second ballot choices for voters that did not choose them on the first ballot.

Voters often lament that they must choose among the lessor of two evils on the November ballot. Third party candidates siphon more votes from one candidate than the other. The Ralph Nader third party candidacy siphoned more votes from Al Gore than George H. W. Bush and that gave the Presidency to Bush rather than Gore in the 2000 election. That lesson is clear in the minds of party leaders and those who would consider a third-party candidacy.

RCV changes that dynamic. If it had been in place in 2000, Al Gore would have become the President. And the Nader candidacy would have been a harmless footnote in American history. RCV eliminates the spoiler effect. That would encourage third party candidates and increase the number of competitive races in the November elections.

Health and Safety Issues

Abortion Rights

The 2022 Supreme Court decision *Dobbs v. Jackson Women's Health Organization* overturned the *Roe v Wade* Supreme Court Decision. A 2022 survey by Pew research Center shows that sixty-one percent say abortion should be legal in all or most cases, while thirty-seven percent say it should be illegal in all or most cases.

The *Roe* position on abortion is typical of other countries around the world. Several years ago, Supreme Court justice John Paul Stevens wrote *"Perhaps Congress would seldom elect to pattern an American program after a foreign model, but our elected representatives, rather than judges, should decide whether it is wise to do so."*

This is not about being pro-life or pro-choice. It is about who controls lawmaking related to one of our most long-lasting and controversial issues. In this case, the party-over-country faction used the might-makes-right philosophy to invoke its preferred ideology. George Washington, Thomas Jefferson, and Abraham Lincoln all argued against this type of court action. In addition, this court action, promoted by the Christian-right, appears to violate the concept of separation of church and state.

Article I of the Constitution states: *"All legislative Powers herein granted shall be vested in a Congress of the United States, which shall consist of a Senate and House of Representatives."* Only Congress has the power to make laws. Our court system was set up by Article III. That article did not grant power to make laws to the United States Supreme Court. Both *Roe* and *Dobbs* were court rulings that effectively created law regarding a woman's reproductive rights. Congress has treated the issue like it was too hot to manage. In 1776, one-third of the colonists opposed the Revolutionary War. What if our elected representatives had treated the issue of declaring our independence from England as too hot to manage?

One might say that their decision to let the issue slide over to the Supreme Court was cowardly. At the very least, Congress passed up the opportunity.

Nineteen applications for an Article V convention have dealt with the abortion issue. Since 1973 we have tolerated a court ruling as doctrine on one of the most controversial issues of our time. Reproductive rights have never been subject to a national vote or decided by our elected representatives. The court is the wrong place for lawmaking. Government should either make law by use of its mandated lawmaking body or get out of the way. Often people complain about government intrusion into our lives. If government representatives elected by the people are unable to legislate rules on the issue, then industry professionals should decide the issue.

It is possible for an organization of medical professionals to establish national policy on reproductive rights. Adequate precedent exists in this country and other peer countries around the world. The organization could establish ethical guidelines. The court system, without laws to the contrary, could follow those guidelines.

Amendments to the Constitution have dealt with controversial issues in the past. For example, The Thirteenth Amendment abolished slavery. We may choose to amend the Constitution for the purpose of defining reproductive rights. It could create either industry-based law, or law by the people's representatives. In either case, the amendment would overturn the will of the nine unelected judges on the United States Supreme Court.

The amendment may set a sunset date in the future. Congress may choose to pass a national reproductive rights law prior to that sunset date, with approval by the President, or the issue would fall to health industry professionals without government interference. Nothing would prevent Congress from acting before or after the sunset date. The amendment would force Congress to act or leave the industry alone with no interference from the court system.

Second Amendment Rights

For weeks prior to the start of the Revolutionary War, British troops were traversing the Massachusetts countryside in attempt to confiscate gunpowder from the American colonists. They were trying to take away our guns so that we could not mount an armed resistance to British authority. Their march on Lexington and Concord was an attempt to take weapons from a storage area. The colonists had no standing army. Resistance was from citizen's militias. Militia forces were a major part of the American resistance to the British.

Twelve years later we drafted our Constitution in Philadelphia. Each of the delegates had clear memories of the contribution to the war by citizen's militias. Aside from the First Amendment and its freedom of speech provisions, historical context suggests that national defense was second on the agenda (hence the second amendment). Our military strength was miniscule as compared to world powers of the day such as France and England.

Our standing army was only seven hundred men while the potential number of state militia troops was many times that number. National defense was very dependent on regulated militias. The convention delegates wanted to make sure that the state and or federal governments would not inhibit the function of this critical national defense force. But writing the Second Amendment caused controversy. Would the states or the federal government control the well-regulated militias? As a result, the wording of the Second Amendment was deliberately vague, and this vague language allowed the amendment to pass.

We have no record of any conversations among the delegates that addressed the concept of a right to bear arms for personal defense. It is most likely that the conversations did not occur because there was adequate precedent that provided an opportunity for a person to defend himself or herself with whatever weapons were at hand. There was simply no need to pass a constitutional amendment to define this opportunity. It is also possible that the delegates discussed and tabled the matter for lack of interest. Or they may have intentionally left it up to the states because there was no need to mandate a national policy that would overrule differing state laws.

The Second Amendment states: *"A well-regulated Militia, being necessary to the security of a Free State, the right of the people to keep and bear Arms, shall not be infringed."*

Note that the militia was to be necessary for the security of a free state, with no reference to individual self-defense protection. The words also have a strong implication that the privately owned weapons were of use to the militia, with no other implied use. The Second Amendment codified our best chance for national defense in a world with much larger, potentially adversarial military powers.

In 1876, the United States Supreme Court ruled that the right to bear arms was NOT a right provided by the Constitution. Prior to 2008 and the *Heller* decision, Congress passed no laws dealing with an individual's right to bear arms for self-defense.

People may use weapons for killing. When we create law or rule that we have the right to bear arms for self-defense, we imply that we have the right to kill each other. Indirectly, laws or rulings that allow killing of a human being, for any reason, go against the moral principle of 'thou shalt not kill.' Our society finds no conflict when we kill during wartime. But conscience may otherwise restrain us from pointing a loaded gun at a person. For 219 years court rulings never concluded that the Second Amendment gave us the right to bear arms for personal defense. Indirectly, the earlier courts may have chosen to not advocate pointing a loaded gun at a person in a non-wartime situation. Today's court should consider that the lack of rulings in the past may have set precedent as a moral decision by those prior courts.

In *Heller*, the court decided that an individual has the right to bear arms for personal defense. The words of the Constitution do not support that premise. Article III of the Constitution only allows the Supreme Court to address cases arising under the Constitution. This leaves the *Heller* decision in a gray area. Gray areas are often subject to party-over-country bias. It seems that the opinion of judges that supported the *Heller* decision reflects the position of gun lobby, not jurisprudence or conscience.

It is obvious that the Republican Party would receive help from expanded gun rights because they have received massive support from gun rights organizations. The National Rifle Association reports that forty-four percent of Republicans own guns and twenty percent of Democrats own guns. The five judges appointed by Republican Presidents voted 5-4 in favor of the decision. Celebration of the *Heller* and later *MacDonald* decisions continue to this day. They have been weaponized (pun intended) by the Republican Party and have created a gun worshiping pseudo-cult. Effectively, the court has carried water for a political ideology. As a result, the bottom-line consequences to the country are very disturbing. Weapons stand for violence. This gives political leaders the opportunity to use this as a side benefit to instill chaos and move the country closer to autocracy.

It is about supporting a political ideology. It is a means to an end, not jurisprudence driven by precedent and conscience.

Congress banned assault weapons from 1994 to 2004. That slowed the gun cult momentum. Gun sales in the United States totaled 7.7 million in 2004 and 29,569 people died from gun violence. The Heller decision occurred in 2008. That year saw 9.6

million guns sales and 31,593-gun deaths occurred. Gun sales and gun violence increased on an irregular basis over the next years. With 21.6 million guns sales in 2021, gun deaths increased to 48,832. The increase in gun violence is closely related to the increase in gun purchases. The incidence of gun deaths increased by fifty-five percent since the *Heller* decision.

Research from Stanford University reviewed U.S. mass shootings over a thirty-five-year period. Although the data may be subject to additional interpretation, a forty percent decrease in mass shooting deaths occurred during the ten-year assault weapons ban. Additionally, the research found that in the decade after the ban expired, mass shooting deaths increased substantially.

The pro-gun position of right-wing politicians has deliberately created an issue driven by passion. Vote harvesting due to this passion has been extraordinarily successful. Deliberate reasoning tells us that assault weapons have no recreational purpose. When passion replaces deliberate reasoning, it weakens our representative democracy.

To be clear, the judges on the Supreme Court did not ask people to go out and buy guns and they did not make any statements in favor of gun violence. But they did lay the groundwork for those that promote gun use. They intentionally or inadvertently created momentum for the expansion of the right-wing gun culture. Close adherence to the non-delegation doctrine would have mandated that Congress make gun laws, not judges. The *Heller* decision set off a firestorm of unforeseen consequences.

A constitutional amendment could overturn *Heller* and ban assault rifles. Other gun regulations laws would fall to Congress or the states.

A 2019 Gallop poll asked the following question: Do you think it should be legal or illegal to manufacture, sell, or possess high-capacity semi-automatic rifles such as the AR-15, AK-47 or M16? Americans favored the ban by sixty-two percent to thirty six percent.

Note that the survey implies that a person could not keep the guns that they already own. And it implies that the federal government could take away twenty million guns, even searching private homes for them. This brings up the question, who would pay for these searches? Or how would our quiet enjoyment of life be damaged if there were conflicts related to taking away those guns?

By just banning the sale and use of the guns, no searches would take place. The resale value of the guns would be the 'black market' value, but the ATF (the government) would not traverse the country to confiscate legally purchased weapons. We may define use as carrying the weapon in a public place, in a vehicle traveling in a public place, or public display of the weapon, including on a media format.

The differing rules on possession may increase the number of people that would favor the sale and use ban as opposed to the possession, sale, and use ban.

Health Care

In 1800, when life expectancy was about forty years, there was no need for a public health care system. Our agrarian society of that day had little access to medical services. And few health care services were available. It was a private pay system with little or no health insurance. Socialized medicine was not an option.

In 1960, life expectancy in the US was about sixty-nine years. Public health care systems were developing around the world, but private health care systems still dominated. As an industry experiences major expansion, its systems need major updating. Today's life expectancy is about ten years longer. This added life span requires a disproportionate amount of added health care. It is not only better treatments and better drugs. A bigger industry requires more management. Costs and services increased.

We may compare our health care system to a large corporation. Good management and successful innovation lead to the best financial outcomes. The difference is that instead of a board of directors of a large corporation, the government determines our type of health care system. Our government chooses whether we have universal health care or a privately run system. That is a management decision. The

United States is the only one of all thirty-six OECD (Organization for Economic Cooperation and Development) nations that do not have universal health care either in practice or by constitutional right.

The best measure of success is comparing our health care system to that of other countries. Comparing health care outcomes, our system is no better or worse, but our costs are higher. We have failed to innovate. It is an unnecessary economic burden.

Our continued lack of universal health care favors corporations. If we adopt universal health care, corporate health industry profits will decrease. When media pundits bad-mouth any government program that does not agree with their ideology, they are being disingenuous at best and anti-democratic at worst. The seven countries that rank highest on the Happiness Index all have more socialistic programs such as universal health care and better access to higher education. If we have the aspirational goals of life, liberty, and the pursuit of happiness, then we should consider pursuing policies that are in line with other developed nations.

Corporations and the wealthy have drawn battle lines against universal health care. They call it socialism with the implication that it is a horror from a dystopian novel. But it is a benefit not a horror.

What the opponents are not telling us is that socialistic programs are a practical choice in various aspects of government. Our interstate highway system is socialistic. It would be more expensive if each municipality had to build its own roads. Government funding for our school system is socialistic. It would be a great burden to our country if we all had to shop for teaching materials and home-school our children. The Postal Service is socialistic. Mailing a letter would be more expensive and less efficient if each post office set its own postal rates.

All governments have a degree of socialism. It is a choice. We can let market forces decide our services or choose government supervision. No government has one-hundred percent socialism or one-hundred percent capitalism. Cost, efficiency, and quality are major concerns of any government service. All other developed nations have chosen universal health care. Not one of them aspires to change their system to our system. We should not be so self-absorbed that we do not learn from other successful health care systems.

Of the G-7 nations, (France, Italy, Great Britain, Japan, Germany, Canada, and the United States), our life expectancy in 2023 was 4.0 years shorter than the other six nations. Our substandard health care system may be part of the reason that people live longer in other countries.

Corporate interests are self-serving. Unlike member of the United States Congress or state legislators, corporations have not taken an oath to support the Constitution. They may not favor the best interests of the citizens of the United States. They see Obamacare and Medicare as an unnecessary shift of wealth from the well-off to the middle and lower classes. They tell us that we should rely on market forces to deal with issues such as health care.

But market forces are not the only consideration. There is a moral and ethical obligation for a nation to take care of its people.

A January 2023 Gallup Poll showed that fifty-seven percent support universal health care.

A 2019 Gallup poll found that twenty-five percent of Americans say they or a family member have delayed medical treatment for a major illness due to cost of care. An estimated 25,000 Americans die each year because they lack health care insurance coverage. We often do not measure the increased stress caused by financial concerns related to medical care in this country. Medical debt is the number one reason for bankruptcy in the United States. Universal health care would eliminate medical bankruptcy.

In his book *Which Country Has the World's Best Health Care?* Ezekiel Emanuel points out deficiencies in our health care system. Only ninety-one percent of Americans have coverage while most every other country has ninety-nine percent coverage. The United States spends twenty-seven percent more per person than the next most expensive country and fifty percent more than most countries.

Emanuel compared health care systems in eleven countries: the United States, Australia, Canada, China, France, Germany, Netherlands, Switzerland, Norway, Taiwan, and United Kingdom. The choice of countries was based on differences related to financing and delivery systems, American familiarity with the country, and those countries that claim to have the best health care systems. He compares eight aspects of their health care systems: history, coverage, financing, payment, delivery of care, prescription drug regulation, human resources, and future challenges. Of the eleven countries, top tier performers were Germany, Netherlands, Norway, and Taiwan. The United States underperformed across most dimensions. Only China has a lower ranking.

Some argue that universal health care could increase the national debt. Data from all other countries show that the total cost of medical services with universal health care is lower not higher. We have zero reason to give away medical services and add the cost to the national debt. We just need to properly channel our resources.

Billionaires have spent decades hammering on the thought that the word 'taxes' is the vilest word in the dictionary. The passion created by their campaign has been remarkably successful at getting votes. The real source of the argument is greed. Fairness is subjective. Branding universal health care as increased taxation dupes the public into voting against a more cost-effective government policy.

Opponents have not fully vetted all the options. They often criticize the Canadian system. But Emanuel does not rate that system in the top tier of systems. The German system rates higher and is structurally different. We should use deliberate reasoning and examine the options before we conclude that all other countries are wrong, and we are right.

A Constitutional amendment could mandate universal health care, but Congress would choose among the alternative universal health care systems.

First Amendment Restrictions

Freedom of speech is one of America's greatest assets. But when that speech shows complete disregard for the health and well-being of others while it clearly gains power or financial advantage for organized interests that disseminate the information, it violates basic American values.

At a crowded Christmas party in Calumet, Michigan in 1913, someone allegedly yelled fire. As a result, many people died. It is legally accepted that you cannot yell fire in a crowded room as part of our First Amendment rights.

Partisan media outlets stated or implied that people should not get the Covid-19 vaccine. Evidence shows that these networks directly or indirectly caused thousands of people to die while campaign donations increased for one political party. Throwing shade on evidence of climate change ignores the increase in heat related deaths worldwide. The fossil fuels industry profits from climate change denial.

We should restrict First Amendment rights as part of the aspirational intent spelled out in our Declaration of Independence. It states that we should *"institute new Government, laying its foundation on such principles and organizing its powers in such form, as to them shall seem most likely to affect their Safety and Happiness."*

Available information shapes our political views. Prior to radio and television, our main news sources were newspapers and word-of-mouth. Mega-media players did not control the political slant of newspapers.

Our partisan divide is hurting our country. Fitch Ratings recent downgrade of American securities (increasing our cost of doing business) was related to partisan bickering in Congress. Increasingly partisan media outlets enhance the level of bickering.

The history of our partisan divide is pertinent to the underlying cause and potential solution to the problem. In 1949, as radio and television became more widely used, the Federal Communications Commission (FCC) instituted the Fairness Doctrine.

The Fairness Doctrine mandated that broadcast networks devote time to contrasting views on issues of public importance and provide balanced and honest coverage. Congress backed the policy in 1954 and by the 1970s the FCC called the doctrine the *"single most important requirement of operation in the public interest – the sine qua non* (an indispensable and essential action, condition, or ingredient) *for grant of a renewal of license."* The Federal Communications Commission (which were all Reagan appointees) abolished the doctrine in 1987. Reagan vetoed a congressional attempt to codify the doctrine.

The doctrine never applied to cable TV or the internet and might not be an appropriate method of oversight today. However, the intent of our Congress was set aside, and we now have little or no media oversight. Misinformation and outright propaganda now go unchecked. Honesty is often missing in today's coverage.

The FCC ended the Fairness Doctrine in 1987. The Rush Limbaugh show premiered in 1988. Fox News and MSNBC premiered in 1996. Voting patterns show that the repeal of the Fairness Doctrine unleashed a powerful wave of legalized media propaganda.

Wikipedia data shows voting results from prior Presidential elections. We can measure a state's partisanship versus the national average with this data. The results are revealing.

In the ten elections from 1960 through 1996, the range of partisanship per state ranged from 8.3 per cent in 1960 to 11.7 per cent in 1964 with an average of 10.2 per cent. The 1996 level was slightly above average at 10.8 per cent. In 1996, Rush Limbaugh was popular on the radio, but Fox News and MSNBC had started only a few months prior to the election.

In 2000, the measure of partisanship jumped to 14.1%. That is significantly above the highest level in the previous forty years. In this election, Fox News, which was available in fifty-six million homes nationwide, saw a staggering 440% increase in viewers, the biggest gain among the three cable news television networks.

By 2002, Fox News became the highest rated news network. In 2004 the states' partisan deviation from the national norm was at 14.4%. In 2008, it jumped to 15.7%.

The *Heller* decision in 2008 may have fanned the flames of radicalism. The 2010 *Citizens United* ruling added dark money and more wealthy donors. In 2012, the partisanship level jumped to 17.4%. In 2016, the partisanship level increased to 17.6%. And it increased again to 18.2% in 2020.

A Pew Research Center study completed in 2017 confirms that the partisan divide over political values was steady prior to the year 2000 and then steadily increased.

The increases coincide with the beginning of the biased reporting of Fox News and MSNBC. Since they became relevant in 2000, all six Presidential elections showed a much higher level of voting bias than all ten of the previous elections. And it is scary that the trend shows a steady increase.

The data clearly shows that media outlets shape and degree of radicalization of our political views. The Fairness Doctrine had a positive influence on keeping partisanship at acceptable levels. Our government discarded the Fairness Doctrine because it did not deal with the ever-increasing number of media influences. But, if we want to reduce the level of partisanship, we may consider restricting media outlets and resurrecting the principles of the Fairness Doctrine. Our media outlets, in their ordinary search for reasonable profits, should not expand our differences of opinion.

Exposure to information from all sources creates a person's political opinion. Innate logic and analysis filter the information. Election results data support the assertion that many Americans do not have an effective ability to filter biased data provided by media outlets. Political messaging, instead of logic and conscience, often creates votes.

Media outlets now have less incentive for balanced coverage. Pundits laugh at opposing views. Ideologies congregate into media bubbles.

The Fairness Doctrine was about fairness between competing ideologies. But removing it not only separated ideologies into opposing media outlets, but it also opened the door to unchecked dissemination of falsehoods.

Joseph Goebbels would be proud of radical American news outlets. He was the propaganda minister for the Nazi Party from 1933 to 1945 and was adept at using new media for propaganda purposes. Philosophically he embraced racism and rejected government based on science and reason. Some of our media outlets embrace the same philosophy. Today, some media outlets treat the First Amendment as an FCC-endorsed propaganda license. That is the opposite of what the FCC intended with the Fairness Doctrine that was in effect between 1949 and 1987.

We define propaganda as dissemination of facts, arguments, rumors, half-truths, and lies to influence public opinion. Currently, propaganda is legal. The First Amendment protects this legal right.

Media polarization creates voter polarization. And that relationship may be stronger and more consequential than we realize. We just do not have the ability to filter out the biased nature of the information that we encounter. And there is no way to compromise with falsehoods. Ever expanding polarization will lead to government threatening consequences.

Radical elected representatives are the result of radical media outlets and not by actions of well-intended voters. Bob Dylan wrote the song 'Only a Pawn in their Game' after witnessing the result of a racially motivated murder in Mississippi. He blamed the system, not the murderers. Today right-wing and left-wing media bubbles control the game. If we want to reduce the partisan divide and avoid overly biased leadership, we must change the rules of the game.

The last time that Congress voted on whether to have a degree of control over the media, it voted in favor of that control. In a devilish twist of fate, the contemptible media actions unleashed by the veto of that legislation changed the landscape. The change in rules resulted in the election of members of Congress that no longer favor any level of control of the media. It is hard to put the evil genie back in the bottle.

The only way to reduce voter polarization is to reduce media polarization. We must restrain the most radical and controversial elements of the media. We should protect the people from propaganda that threatens our health or our system of government. Our Founders stated the aspirational goal of protecting our safety. And our lawmakers swore an oath to protect our Constitution. Organized dissemination of falsehoods that harm Americans or our system of government, for the purpose of profit and power, should be illegal.

Does freedom of speech also mean freedom of corporate speech? Rules of our society do not obligate corporations to protect and defend the United States Constitution. When their speech, with the sole intent of increasing profits, hurts others or hurts our government, we should restrain that speech.

Some of the leaders of the January 6th, 2021, insurrection have been convicted of seditious conspiracy. Right wing media outlets may have contributed to the conspiracy by claiming or

49

implying that a biased government stole the 2020 presidential election. That falsehood indirectly threatened our government. Sedition is legally defined in18 U.S. Code § 2383 - Rebellion or insurrection. It states in part *"Whoever incites, sets on foot, assists, or engages in any rebellion or insurrection against the authority of the United States or the laws thereof, or gives aid or comfort thereto..."*

We may interpret election denial as rebelling against the authority and laws of the United States. The news outlets had unambiguous evidence that the results of the election were not in dispute. Seditious actions by media outlets should not be able to hide behind absolute freedom of speech and profit from those actions.

Organizing and disseminating falsehoods for power or profit is wrong when it threatens the safety of the people or the continuation of our government. Falsehoods should not physically harm other people and should not be a tool to advocate insurrection against the government.

On the contrary, individual speech, expressing a falsehood, is less likely to be harmful.

The insurrection failed. But the underlying factors that fomented that insurrection are still in place. We have an increasingly larger partisan gap. Our First Amendment still protects propaganda. Complete repeal of the Fairness Doctrine is a contributing underlying cause.

A new amendment to the Constitution would be necessary to restrict the First Amendment

Other Functional Flaws

Term Limits on Supreme Court Justices

We are the only country on earth that gives lifetime tenure to Supreme Court judges without a mandatory retirement age. Of the over eight hundred constitutions adopted worldwide since 1787, none give similar lifetime tenure. Few institutions of any kind have adopted the rule of lifetime appointment. The experience of other democracies is relevant to our own institutional design. James Madison studied examples from other countries prior to writing the Constitution. The average term for term-limited judges in other countries is nine years. A Chris Kahn study showed that sixty-three percent of Americans favored term or age limits on Supreme Court justices. In 2022, an Associated Press NORC poll found that sixty-seven percent of Americans believe that justices should have to step down after a specific number of years. We have bantered about the concept of an eighteen-year term limit on Supreme Court justices in academic circles in this country. Both conservatives and progressives favor the idea.

Term limits set at eighteen years would take air out of the political football. Each President would get to nominate two judges per term.

For over two hundred years, the Senate has given advice and consent to the President's nominees for the Supreme Court. We accepted that the power to nominate rested with the President and not the Senate. Recently, the Senate has exercised veto power over the nomination. The words in the Constitution and centuries of precedent do not lead us to think that the leaders of the Senate have the power to block a President's nomination to the Supreme Court. This is a flaw in our system of government. It is either one way or the other. There is no half-way. Either the Senate or the President have the ultimate power. The evidence points to the necessity of codifying the President's right to select Supreme Court justices. The Senate would still give advice and consent, just like it has done for many decades.

With eighteen-year term limits, there would no longer be any incentive to nominate young judges so that a political ideology could advance for added years. It would be best if the age of the nominee would ensure that the nominee would serve during his or her most productive years; after gaining adequate experience, and before old age would reduce productivity.

In a paper called Term Limits and Turnover on the US Supreme Court: Tom Ginsberg wrote a Comparative View, and he testified for the

Presidential Commission on the Supreme Court on July 20, 2021. He noted that almost half of our Supreme Court justices have died in office. Time spent on the bench averaged 14.9 years prior to 1970 and 25.3 years since then. Most of this difference can be attributed to longer life expectancy in recent decades.

Death of a Supreme Court judge should not give one party an advantage and one party a disadvantage. Retirement of a judge should not be politically motivated. With two appointments per presidential term, the nomination would belong to the party that won the presidency for that term. A political party could no longer steal a nomination. No amount of stalling by a Senate led by an opposing party could take the nominating opportunity away from the party of the President.

An amendment to the Constitution is necessary to limit the term of Supreme Court justices.

Secret Impeachment Votes

From time-to-time Congress may decide that a President of the United States has done wrong. Impeachment proceedings tend to become overly political. Whether the votes are in a House committee, the whole House of Representatives, or for removal from office in the Senate, members vote for or against the President.

Those who vote against the wishes of party leaders fear risking the loss of standing in that party. They could lose committee assignments or face primary election challenges from within the party. Party pressure causes the votes to be strictly along party lines. But the true intent of the vote is to decide guilt or innocence of President. Individual members of Congress, under ideal circumstances, decide based on their own private conclusions, not party mandates. This party loyalty problem has become obvious in all recent impeachment votes. In 1974 it was not a major issue in the impeachment proceedings against Richard Nixon. Excessive polarization has changed the political landscape since then.

Recent impeachment and removal proceedings show that individual members of Congress have lost their status because they voted against party leadership. This is a flaw in the Constitution. We need to hear dissenting voices or else we could never impeach a President and remove them from office unless the two-thirds or more of the Senate were members of the opposing party. That situation has not occurred in recent history. The opposition party has always held more than one-third of Senate seats.

This situation gives the President unwarranted power. Substantial wrongdoing, and even criminal conduct by the President is viewed through a party-first lens.

There may be an antidote. If the vote were secret, no member of either party would see who voted for or against the interests of the President. Retaliation against a member voting their conscience, and not voting the party line, would not be possible. We should let the consequences match the level of transgression and reduce this unwarranted presidential power.

An amendment to the Constitution is necessary to mandate secret impeachment votes.

Accidently Gerrymandered Senate

The Senate gives equal representation to each state regardless of population. States with smaller populations tend to elect Republican Senators and states with larger populations tend to elect Democrats. The population difference between large states and smaller states is large. If all the smaller states collectively voted, they could obtain a Senate majority and at the same time represent only twenty-five percent of the nation's population.

Half of the nation's population, enough electoral college votes to win the presidency, resides in only fourteen states. These fourteen states can cast only twenty-eight votes in the Senate when fifty or fifty-one are necessary to have a Senate majority.

Much of the real power in the Senate is controlled by states with small populations. Our Founder's intent was to make sure that the smaller states were fully represented. But this system does not protect states with large populations from domination in the Senate by states with smaller populations. This becomes a significant issue when a major partisan divide separates the country and when the ideological divide shows itself as small states of one party versus large states of the other party. This has occurred often in recent years.

The Senate alone confirms judges to the Supreme Court. Until 2017, a sixty to forty majority of Senators was necessary to confirm an appointment. Only a simple majority is necessary today. The Senate confirmed the last three Supreme Court justices with Senators whose constituencies consisted of less than half of the population of the United States. The votes were strict party-line votes. Prior to 2017, members of both parties usually confirmed Supreme Court nominees.

This 2017 'nuclear option' was a dangerous cancellation of the precedents that protected all Americans from the rouge court decisions of biased judges. Recent court decisions have since widened our partisan divide.

We have little remedy for a sitting biased judge, but we can do things to compensate for the 2017 breech in precedent. We should prevent the small states from unnecessarily dominating the large states.

Amending the Constitution and preventing action by Senators representing a minority of Americans is the only way to correct the problem.

To prevent small states from dominating the confirmation of Supreme Court judges, we may require that Senators whose constituents are more than half of Americans approve each nominee.

Often, that will require votes from both political parties just like prior to 2017.

The new amendment would acknowledge that moving away from the long-held precedent of bipartisan support for Supreme Court judges is not in this country's best interest. In many cases, the new amendment would cause the President to appoint judges that have ideologies that are more moderate and avoid judges that are highly party oriented.

Lame-Duck Pardons

Michael Flynn, Roger Stone, Paul Manafort, and Steve Bannon may have committed crimes that interfered with our national security. Yet while they were committing those acts, they had reasonable assurance from the President that our justice system would never hold them accountable for their actions. Each received a presidential pardon.

The pardons occurred after the President had lost the election and before the President had left office. Other Presidents have issued questionable lame-duck pardons. If we end the President's power to issue pardons during this lame-duck period, the President's pardon power would still be in place for ninety-five percent of the presidential term. And all pardons issued by the President would be subject to the scrutiny of the voters in the next election.

Ending this political gimmickry would instill greater confidence in the institution of the Presidency and protect national security.

A constitutional amendment is necessary to adjust the President's pardon power.

Fix Article V

This new amendment would create a new and easier path to amending the United States Constitution. It is also a calculated response to the rising tide of competitive authoritarianism created by those who claim to have a monopoly on reason.

If we wish to satisfy the aspirations of our Founders, we may consider amending Article V. Instead of lobbyists, political parties, and media influence dominating our national reform agenda, we may seek to insert public opinion. Rather than a convention and untrustworthy delegates, we may streamline the process by allowing thirty-eight state legislatures to have the complete power to amend the Constitution.

And in each state voters might choose, by meeting a minimum threshold, to have a statewide vote on an issue dealing with amending the United States Constitution. After this advisory vote, the state legislature must have an up or down vote on the issue. Approval by this timely vote would be ratification of the amendment by that state. If the voters choose not to have the advisory vote (unnecessary statewide votes can be expensive), the state legislature may vote to approve the amendment.

The proposed statewide advisory votes are not a major change to state protocols. In forty-nine states, to modify a state constitution, at least one form of ballot measure is mandatory.

A moderate period may occur after the advisory referendum vote and before the final legislative action. This would allow national vetting and refining of the amendment language. After the moderate period, say six months, the state legislature must vote, even if they did not like the message sent by the voters.

This 'Fix Article V' amendment would eliminate some potential legal challenges. Adopting other new amendments may be easier and more reflective of public opinion. It appeals to moral authority and would encourage a more functional government by bringing the opinions of the people into the government reform process. Those who oppose it may give the impression that they oppose a functional representative democracy.

Discussion of this amendment would inform state legislators of their potential role in amending the Constitution and bring national civics discussion to the dinner table. Dark money, political parties, and the media may have to take a back seat on the issues.

With most state ballot initiatives or referendums, the result is final. That state must use the results of the statewide vote. That sends an important message but still lacks one piece of the puzzle. Potentially we have the interests of the legislators on one side and the opinions of the people on the other side. But there is little further debate or discussion. If we have a statewide advisory vote on a proposed Constitutional amendment, discussion on the issue may continue. The news cycle may not end right after the vote tally. Each side will want to justify its position prior to the mandated vote by the legislature. This is a healthy result. Voters may judge their elected representatives based on the reaction of those representatives to the state-wide vote. Debating divergent interests strengthens our government.

Adopting new amendments and debate over the issues may change the makeup of Congress and our state legislatures. Those favoring country-over-party may gain seats from those who place personal and corporate interests over the interests of the people. That political shift would increase the opportunity to create a social safety net that would be more like those in other developed countries. Issues dealing with climate change may receive more attention. Indirectly, new amendments may reduce incarceration rates and high gun death rates. Outlying ideologies would have less influence. With a better system of checks and balances, corporations would have less influence.

This is a direct democracy influence only. It is not a national referendum. That would be direct democracy. With the 'Fix Article V' amendment, the ultimate power would remain with the state legislatures.

Summary

The last time that we proposed and adopted an amendment to the United States Constitution was in 1971. For each of the fourteen issues discussed above, the problems have developed or increased in recent decades. New amendments can address these issues.

Other Concerns

Taxes and Wealth

Income allows a family to get by; wealth allows a family to get ahead. In a 2020 article on wealth inequality by Ana Hernandez Kent, she noted wealth distribution statistics for 1989 and 2016. The top ten percent increased their wealth in this period while the middle class and lower class lost wealth. Clearly the top ten percent have gotten richer on the backs of the middle class and the poor.

Taxation and wealth distribution have changed since the 1960's and 1970's. When measuring wealth accumulation, the lower fifty percent of Americans have accumulated only one percent of the wealth. An article by accountlearning.com about income inequality says, "*Political democracy is only a far-fetched dream in a country where there are gross inequalities of income.*" Non-wealthy Americans have limited structural barriers preventing them from being upwardly mobile. But economic barriers are pervasive and onerous. We are no longer the land of opportunity.

Corporate policy seems to revolve around the

concept of just giving workers or employees enough money so they can survive and keep working. Lack of upward mobility has been a cause of frustration and angst toward the government.

In 2013, Robert Reich wrote 'Four decades ago, the typical household's income rose in tandem with output. But since the late 1970s, as these (supply-side) laws took hold, most Americans' incomes have flattened. Had the median household income continued to keep pace with economic growth it would now be almost $92,000 instead of $50,000.'

From 1932 to 1981 the highest tax rate for high income earners varied from sixty-three percent to ninety-four percent. With supply side economic theory, the rate dropped to fifty percent in 1982, dropped below forty percent in 1987, and has stayed under forty percent since that time. In 2018, the Internal Revenue Service lowered the capital gains rate for investors to twenty-one percent; the lowest rate in 68 years.

Corporations have also seen a recent decline in tax rates. From 1951 to 1969 the highest corporate tax rates were above fifty percent. From 1970 to 1986 the rates gradually declined to forty-six percent. The highest tax rate was thirty-nine percent till 2017. Since 2017, the maximum corporate tax rate has been twenty-one percent.

Supply-side is what George H.W. Bush once called voodoo economics. This 'trickle down' economic theory gave corporations more money, more power, and more influence in our political system. Candidates that they supported indirectly led to the *Citizens United* Supreme Court ruling that gave corporations even greater power and political influence.

We learned that when we cut taxes for the rich, they keep the tax cuts. And we must make up for that lost revenue by increasing taxes or reducing benefits for everyone else. The federal government's contribution to education and infrastructure has suffered. In 1969, an eighteen-year-old, with no unique skills, could work a summer job in a Detroit factory and earn enough money to pay for room and board, tuition, and books, for one year at an in-state university. Today, that is not possible.

With more money in the hands of fewer, those wealthy individuals obtained more power. While supply-side economics is not itself a corrupt economic theory, the results of decades of this economic policy set us up for corruption. Those with a propensity for greed and lust for power found a home.

A lawmaker's goal would logically be to simultaneously maximize economic efficiency and satisfaction of the constituents. The goal of the wealthy and corporations is just to maximize economic efficiency with little or no concern for the happiness of the people. The difference causes this country to have unique social problems.

High Incarceration Rates

Out of the two hundred countries with available data, the United States has the highest incarceration rate in the world at 629 prisoners per 100,000 of population (2023 data). Comparing us to our most relevant comparable countries, the other six of the G-7 nations, we have over six times as many prisoners per capita. Their rates range from a low of eighty-seven in Japan to 159 in Great Britain.

The Prison Policy Initiative argues that incarceration dehumanizes poor people and minorities and does not actually increase public safety. As we search for reasons for this blight on American society, we find that our system of government also stands out in one respect. As we examine the gradient that measures the degree of capitalism versus the degree of socialism in government, we find that we are one of the most capitalistic countries in the world. It is easy to conclude that our intentional rejection of socialistic policy at every turn has led to high crime rates and the resulting high incarceration rates. Governments that have better social safety nets have less crime and incarceration.

People say that power corrupts, and absolute power corrupts absolutely. The fossil fuels industry shows us an important example. If you read "Blowout" by Rachel Maddow, you will find details of corruption around the world that are often closely related to the wealth created by fossil fuels.

Wherever the fossil fuel industry dominates the economy, corruption increases. Today's Russia stands out as a good example. Its oil company profits have led to a government best described as a kleptocracy (where the rulers steal the country's resources). In this country and other countries, areas dominated by the fossil fuels industry have little use for socialistic safety net programs.

The 'oil patch' representatives in Congress represent the power of the fossil fuels industry. They keep that power because voters do not want to lose the jobs created by that industry. If it is true that the incarceration rate is related to the lack of a social safety net, then we may expect the 'oil patch' states to have higher incarceration rates. The two states with the highest incarceration rates, Louisiana, and Oklahoma, are in the middle of the oil patch states. And the sixteen states with highest incarceration rates (as of 2018) each had legislatures controlled by the party aligned with the fossil fuels industry.

As early as the 1830's, advocates saw universal education as one way to end poverty, crime, and other social problems. Early leaders argued that the costs of properly educating children in public schools would be far less than the expenses of punishing and jailing criminals and coping with problems stemming from poverty. About forty-seven percent of public-school revenues come from the state level, forty-five percent from the local level, and eight percent from the federal level. The twenty-two states with the least funding per pupil in 2022 all had Republican state legislatures.

High Gun Death Rates

We have 6.5 times the number of gun deaths per capita as the other six G-7 nations. They had one gun death for every fifteen guns owned and we had one gun death for every eighteen guns owned. That is a consistent rate. The obvious conclusion is that having more guns, results in more gun deaths.

The Declaration of Independence states that we should arrange for our government to achieve *safety* and happiness for its people. Considering our elevated level of gun deaths and our aspirational goals as a nation, it is illogical to promote more gun ownership. Gun deaths reduce our life expectancy by up to two years per person. When the gun lobby and their right-wing supporters promote expansion of gun ownership and expanding gun rights, we may certainly question their desire to promote this nation's best interests.

Assault rifles are at the psychological tip of the spear. Their design is for the sole purpose of killing as many people as possible as quickly as possible. They have no recreational purpose. Mass shootings often involve assault rifles. And, too often, the deaths include innocent children. Those headliner deaths are unacceptable to a vast majority of Americans. A ban on assault rifles would be a big defeat for not only the gun rights supporters but also those that consistently collaborate with them. This psychological victory would end their full control of gun rights policy and send a message to right-wing extremists that the voters are in charge.

Corporate Domination

Each state and federal legislator has sworn an oath to support the Constitution of the United States. If they choose a path that leads to autocratic rule, they have violated a sworn oath. Those who hold positions on a corporate board of directors have not taken that oath. In contrast they typically follow the ideology where self-determination has priority over supporting social well-being. When faced with a choice of oligarchy or representative democracy, self-interest is their guide.

Part of our system of government involves oversight of corporations. But if that oversight fails, greed will overwhelm conscience and we will drift toward corporate oligarchy. Giving away more power, and influence on corporations lowers our ranking on the Democracy Index. That is why the *Citizen's United* ruling is not in the best interests of representative democracy.

Non-Delegation Doctrine

The non-delegation doctrine is a seldom discussed principle of constitutional and administrative law that holds that legislative bodies cannot delegate their legislative powers to executive agencies or private entities. In other words, lawmakers should not allow others to make laws. In the context of the federal government, the doctrine comes from an interpretation of Article I in the United States Constitution and refers to the separation of powers principle. Article I, Section 1 states: *"All legislative Powers herein granted shall be vested in a Congress of the United States, which shall consist of a Senate and House of Representatives."*

A common misunderstanding about the function of the Supreme Court puts air under the wings of the wannabe autocrats. The Founders wanted the court to interpret laws, not make them. Although Supreme Court rulings have the weight of law, it is the job of Congress to make laws, especially where the Constitution does not clearly address the issue. In 1786 the court ruled that we do *not* have the right to bear arms for self-defense in *Cruickshank*. That same body changed the ruling with the *Heller* decision. But neither decision fully follows the Non-Delegation Doctrine. And in both *Roe* and *Dobbs*, according to the Founder's design, Congress should have created the policy, not the Supreme Court. Congressional action should have determined our campaign financing rules, not the *Citizens United* ruling.

Gun rights, abortion rights, and corporate involvement in campaign finance are all issues not clearly spelled out in the Constitution. When we survey the most prominent issues as described by voters, we often find that these social hot-button issues are near the top of the list. Many legislators are elected based on their position on these issues. And then those legislators dodge voting on hot-button issues and let the unelected members of the Supreme Court make the critical decisions. That is not representative democracy. That gives too much power to the judicial branch of government. It also gives the candidates for office free reign to make promises, election after election, about vague general principles, without ever casting a definitive vote.

Those who prefer a more autocratic government want the unelected (potentially biased) judges to effectively become lawmakers. That removes the obligation from our elected representatives in Congress. Currently, we have no effective oversight over an out-of-control court. Our system of checks and balances is not working. With today's 6-3 majority, the court may choose to impose biased ideology on the country without fear of voter's will. Considering the principles of the non-delegation doctrine, this is not what our Founders intended.

Summary

Many issues are not easily addressed by constitutional amendments. For issues such as tax policy, high incarceration rates, high gun death rates, and corporate domination, we hope that better understanding of the autocratic playbook, and voting based on that understanding, will lead to leadership that will deal with these and other critical issues.

Social problems have arisen in recent decades. We need to step back and look at the big picture, look past the perpetual nay-sayers, driven by greed and lust for power, and make government management choices based on deliberate reasoning. This will take a rebirth of political thinking and a strong and persistent desire to improve our government.

The Threat of Autocracy

Part of an article published in the New Yorker in December 2020 states: "The default condition of humankind, traced across thousands of years of history, is some sort of autocracy. The interesting question is not what causes autocracy (not to mention the conspiratorial thinking that feeds it) but what has ever suspended it. The way to shore up American democracy is to strengthen liberal institutions, in ways that are unglamorously specific and discouragingly minute. The temptation of anti-democratic cult politics is forever with us, and so is the work of fending it off. There is no set-it-and-forget-it solution to democratic fragility."

We may disagree that autocracy still is a default position of government in the modern world, but none can deny that it still is a potent competing force. Those parties wishing to move our country in an autocratic direction are likely to have an agenda that includes the following policy goals:

- Media domination
- Voter suppression
- Debate avoidance.

- One party control of the Supreme Court
- Inability to amend the Constitution.
- Climate change denial
- Church and state partnership

Media Domination

Our Founders believed that good government involves taking a learned perspective on each issue and using deliberate reasoning, not passion.

Emotions sell. Passion sells. Sensationalism sells. Extremism sells. Controversy sells.

The profit-motivated media sees the public as kids in a candy store. We choose things that suit our tastes, and not necessarily what we might need to make good personal or political business decisions. We demand instant gratification and look to satisfy our need for gossip and emotional involvement. Science, facts, and discussion of government flaws are less desirable. Profits follow public demand, not the need for useful information.

Those that wish to move our country toward autocracy naturally want to control the media. All dictatorships have media control. Exaggeration, inuendo, misinformation, and conspiracy theories are weapons of the media outlets that favor autocracy.

As Rupert Murdoch, head of Fox News recently said, it is not about red and blue, it is about green. Red refers to red states, blue refers to blue states, and green refers to the American green-back dollar.

Conspiracy theories are like candy. We enjoy hearing them. They are entertaining. It is easy for a media outlet to spin a conspiracy theory into a political controversy. The result is passion, anger, and profit for the media owner. Today's biased media information can easily persuade those of us who go with the flow. Conspiracy theories can be a tool to create votes.

Social media can be especially toxic. The most outrageous comments spread like wildfire. That adds revenue. It cannot be surprising that the owners install algorithms that enhance the number of viewers for these controversial messages. It is passion on-steroids.

Media owner's profit from spreading the message of distrust in government. It is easy to gain viewers by blaming the government for everything that seems wrong. Distrust in government historically has set the table for autocratic government. Recent increases in domestic terrorism and political unrest embolden their interests.

People say that the only time that the press is free is if you own the press. That sentiment deserves attention today. If rich people own the media, their views dominate our information sources. The average person cannot adequately filter all the information. Therefore, our available information leads us to policies established by the rich. And we slide toward plutocracy, government by the rich. That is not representative democracy.

Voter Suppression

The Guardian reported that the advocacy arm of the Heritage Foundation, the powerful conservative think tank based in Washington, spent more than five million dollars on lobbying in 2021 as it worked to block federal voting rights legislation. It was part of an ambitious plan to spread its far-right agenda calling for aggressive voter suppression measures in battleground states.

Every autocratic government engages in voter suppression. The Heritage Foundation is a poster child for right-wing, sometimes anti-democratic, ideology.

Debate Avoidance

Traditionally debates have supplied a useful source of information that voters need to make their choices. The Lincoln-Douglas debates and the Kennedy-Nixon debates are good examples. For the President, press conferences have also been useful. Informed voters make choices based on reasoning.

But, to function well, candidates and the media sponsor must all want to support the goal of informing the public. The media sponsor or candidates can make a mockery of a debate.

Sponsors can agree to debate rules that allow candidates to interrupt each other or run well past their allotted time limit. Candidates can refuse to answer pointed questions by deflecting them and returning to their favorite campaign rhetoric. The debate can turn into a pre-planned showcase for talking points rather than a question-and-answer format. Rude candidates can turn the debate into a shouting match.

The President can poison a press conference. By choosing favored reporters and avoiding others, they can control the narrative. Avoiding regular press conferences robs the voters of information. Town hall meetings are part of the process of informing the public about the issues at hand. Avoiding town hall meetings restricts voter input into the legislative process.

Those who want a more autocratic government have little interest in supplying reliable information to the public. They prefer the mushroom treatment; feed them a little manure and keep them in the dark. An uninformed public is more likely to cast their votes based on misinformation or passion. Well-run debates, regular full press conferences, and town hall meetings threaten their party-over-country ideology.

As part of a partisan agenda Congress avoids debate. Members of Congress talk past each other just to spell out their party's positions but do not respond to words said by the other party.

In 1800, each member of Congress represented about 30,000 people. In 1970 each congressperson represented about 450,000 people. Today it is about 700,000. Staying connected with constituents is harder than it was decades ago. Avoiding the dissemination of information favors the interests of those who lean toward autocratic government.

One-Party Control of the Supreme Court

Whether by random chance or nefarious deed, the Republican Presidents have appointed the most judges on the Supreme Court for more than fifty years. In earlier decades, a bipartisan vote was necessary to confirm court appointments. The necessity of a bipartisan vote (filibuster rule) prompted the President to choose judges that did not promote radical ideology.

So long as both political parties chose to govern in the best interests of the nation and not the best interests of their political party, the appointments to the Supreme Court supported representative democracy. But around the year 2008, the sentiment started to shift. We elected a Democratic non-white President. That caused a racially motivated backlash from the Republican Party. The Republican led Senate began to refuse to confirm lower court judges appointed by the Democratic President. This reprehensible action set off a destructive chain reaction. The President had two bad options. He could wave the white flag and let the opposition party control the entire lower court system or he could remove the filibuster and continue to appoint lower court judges just like prior Presidents had done.

He chose to remove the filibuster on lower court confirmations. That action caused the Republican led Senate to remove the filibuster for appointing Supreme Court judges in 2017. The domino effect, caused by the original reprehensible action, has led to three judges now sitting on the court; each confirmed on a party line vote. No bipartisan votes were necessary.

Resulting votes by the court show that these judges often promote the ideology of the Republican Party over the interests of most Americans. One judge, at the confirmation hearing, said that *Roe* was 'settled law' and later voted to overturn that ruling. Today, the character of the nominee may be a secondary issue. We may now have individuals on the court who take their marching orders from wealthy donors who support radical ideology rather than exercising jurisprudence and acting on behalf of the American people. Impeachment is the only constitutional remedy for inappropriate conduct. That is an absolute joke because sympathetic party members would easily veto that effort. Oversight is lacking.

We are a nation of laws. But laws may be only as good as the judges that interpret those laws. As we looked to free ourselves of the tyranny of King George III, we wrote the Declaration of Independence. In it, the ninth grievance against King George III states *"He has made Judges dependent on his Will alone, for the tenure of their offices, and the amount and payment of their salaries."* We must ask if promotion of the will of one political party was the sole purpose of recent judge appointments and subsequent one-sided confirmation hearings?

Our government was set up with three equal branches of government with checks and balances for each branch. But this has not been true for the United States Supreme Court. In the past twenty-eight years, Democratic voters have cast more votes for President than Republican voters in six of the seven presidential elections. But Republican appointees to the court have had the voting majority for all twenty-eight years. When it comes to court decisions, it is of the people, by the Republican minority, and for the Republican minority. Inability to amend the Constitution, and thus overrule the court, keeps this imbalance in place.

Historically, new amendments to the Constitution have overturned eight Supreme Court decisions. But if we stop amending the Constitution, the judges on the court have effectively become law gods and law goddesses. Without having a method to overturn Supreme Court rulings, as previous generations have done, we have a weakened system of checks and balances. This contributes to the fact that our ratings on the Democracy Index have been in slow decline. That index labels our government as a 'flawed democracy.' We rank 30th out of 167 countries, hardly the shining city on the hill. Canada, Germany, France, Great Britain, and Japan all have higher rankings.

Inability to Amend the Constitution

Amending the Constitution may upset the policy agenda of those driven by a quest for wealth and power. They prefer that the country treats the Constitution as immutable, impossible to change, like the Bible. They attack all efforts to correct government flaws and use words like socialist, liberal, or radical left to demonize those efforts. They endlessly repeat the accusations and emphasize the attack words in each sentence. Those tactics are working. In recent decades, we have not adopted any new amendments.

The Council of State Governments and the National Conference of State Legislators have avoided discussion of new Constitutional amendments. These organizations are in the best position to assist in the implementation of the state-initiated part of Article V. It is not on their radar screen. Is the radar screen influenced by autocratic players?

George Washington said in his Farewell Address that we should use the opinion of the people to correct flaws in our government. This concept is the basis of our representative democracy. If we disconnect the people's ability to alter our government, we are busy dying. And our representative democracy may slide toward oligarchy, plutocracy, or theocracy.

Climate Change

The fossil fuel industry has thrown shade on the green energy industry from the start because that industry competes with oil company profits. They collaborate with the Heritage Foundation and right-wing advocates.

Democrats and Republicans are both affected equally by the increase in carbon dioxide in our atmosphere. The United States has put more carbon in the atmosphere, especially on a per capita basis, than any other country. If we, as a country, side with those that deny and smokescreen the problem, the rest of the world will come to resent us for our inaction.

If we choose the path of self-determination, as corporations and their supporters wish, then we deny the concept that all nations are in this together. Letting fossil fuels companies write our Environmental Protection Agency standards and decide our national policy on climate change is dangerous. Other nations may see this as morally corrupt.

Pure capitalism, when it leads us to decisions on critical international issues, is at best, questionable, and at worst will lead to disaster. We may be stepping outside the long-held guardrails of our democratic republic when we let the short-term interests of American industry threaten the health of future generations and disrupt the long-term stability of international policy.

Anti-government weaponizing of all green efforts is a useful disinformation tool for wannabe autocrats. The 'windmills cause cancer' campaign has been effective. Oil company dogma indirectly leads to corruption in this and other countries around the world.

Church and State Partnership

In 'Dune' written by Frank Herbert in 1965, he quotes an old proverb: "When religion and politics travel in the same cart, the riders believe nothing can stand in their way. Their movement becomes headlong--faster and faster and faster. They put aside all thought of obstacles and forget that the precipice does not show itself to the man in a blind rush until it is too late."

Those on one side of the political aisle have chosen to promote Christian morality while implying that the other party is godless It is a choice to gain more votes. The choice is odd because the principles of Christian faith do not closely align with the morals and actions of that political party. Their leaders do not go to church more often than average Americans. There is no evidence that their wives or daughters have fewer abortions. They often follow the business philosophy of Ayn Rand. Many on the board of directors in major American companies have read her book 'Atlas Shrugged' which promotes self-determination. Ayn Rand was an outspoken atheist. Corporate morality and lessons taught by the Christian faith are not in compliance. Yet both are part of the same party base.

But the alignment makes sense from other perspectives. Faith is a form of passion. Those of us who are prone to critical thinking and deliberate reasoning are often not strongly religious. Voters who act based on passion are more susceptible to propaganda. The Christian church is more like a dictatorship than a democracy. Autocratic messaging is already part of Christian life.

Our Constitutional Challenge

We commonly see the accepted approach to amending the Constitution as studying legal documents, following legal precedents, and then using this information to choose a path. Alternatively, we may define the goal as following the aspirations and writings of our Founders, using the will of the people, and then choosing a path that does not break any laws. The alternative path is wider and gives us more opportunities to correct constitutional flaws.

Scholars often hail our Constitution as a great document. James Madison, often regarded as the author of the Constitution, did extensive research prior to the 1787 Convention. Fifty-five of America's best and brightest men got together for four months and designed a new type of government for its day. It is an experiment in government. Checks and balances were set up for the three branches of government. For over two centuries it has stood the test of time. But our Founders also acknowledged that it was not perfect. Article V of the Constitution allows correction of constitutional flaws. The delegates to the convention even acknowledged that a time might occur when Congress would become intransigent and not make necessary changes. In that case, the states would take the lead in the amendment process.

Since the 1787 convention, we have amended our Constitution seventeen times, which is about once every fourteen years. It has been over fifty years since our last new amendment. This extended gap is significant. Our Congress has become unwilling to address Constitutional flaws, and it is not surprising that the congressional approval rating since 2010 has hovered around a dismal twenty percent.

The recent rise in party-over-country politics is unprecedented in our history. But it is not completely unexpected. In George Washington's Farewell Address, he spoke about the dangers of 'spirit of party.' Paraphrasing his words, he said that party-first politics serves to distract public council, enfeeble the public administration, agitate the community with ill-founded jealousies and false alarms, kindle animosity of one party against another, and foment occasional riot and insurrection. Washington also makes it clear that spirit of party, sharpened by the spirit of revenge, can easily lead to the rise of an autocratic leader.

Lack of congressional action on important matters is a result of our most recent political environment. Party loyalties are getting in the way of the deliberate reasoning necessary to solve national problems. But despite recent fighting between our political parties, we are still a nation of laws. Recent complacency and diminished national spirit should not stop us from seeking corrections to our system of government.

Article V states: *"The Congress, whenever two thirds of both Houses shall deem it necessary, shall propose Amendments to this Constitution, or, on the Application of the Legislatures of two thirds of the several States, shall call a Convention for proposing Amendments, which, in either Case, shall be valid to all Intents and Purposes, as Part of this Constitution, when ratified by the Legislatures of three fourths of the several States, or by Conventions in three fourths thereof, as the one or the other Mode of Ratification may be proposed by the Congress; Provided that no Amendment which may be made prior to the Year One thousand eight hundred and eight shall in any Manner affect the first and fourth Clauses in the Ninth Section of the first Article; and that no State, without its Consent, shall be deprived of its equal Suffrage in the Senate."*

With today's elevated level of animosity between the two parties, party line votes are quite common. Elected representatives seem obligated to vote for the party and disregard their own conscience, the good of the country, or the interest of their constituents. Amendments to the Constitution by use of Congress require a super majority vote. This happened for each of the amendments adopted since 1787. With strict party line votes, and a relatively even split between the two parties, this super majority vote in Congress is not likely.

Our Founders understood the possibility of an uncooperative Congress. But when they drafted Article V, they did not foresee the changing perspective on the possibility of an Article V convention.

The convention method bypasses the United States Congress. At the time that the delegates approved the Constitution, they accepted and commonly used political conventions. In the past one hundred years it has fallen out of favor. Unfortunately, we have no other way to bypass Congress and legally amend the Constitution. We are stuck with words written more than two centuries ago.

History has shown that major corrections to our governmental problems often began with applications to an Article V convention. The states have started, but never successfully completed the process of amending our Constitution. The applications, by the states, have often created momentum. That momentum shifted to Congress thus avoiding the need for a separate convention.

Unfortunately, in recent history, the widening partisan divide has stifled all attempts to correct the flaws in our Constitution.

Examining Our Options

In George Washington's Farewell Address, he said:

"The basis of our political systems is the right of the people to make and to alter their Constitution of Government." Today, those Americans who lean toward autocratic government are making an earnest effort to take away that right. Their messaging strategically avoids all connection to government reforms. The flawed status quo has increased their profits and power.

Are we just sitting by and watching the slow drift toward oligarchy and autocracy that has progressed since the 1960's and 1970's? Should we wave the white flag? Autocrats strive to make this our default position. Our Founders would not have approved. As Tim Snyder said in 'On Tyranny,' *"We have allowed ourselves to accept the politics of inevitability, a self-induced coma, where we assume that history with its seemingly distant traumas of fascism Nazism and Communism are no longer relevant."*

The autocrats and their friends, even though they are a minority, are in the habit of winning battles over tax rates, voting rights, banking regulations, health insurance, election reform, gerrymandering, and the environment. Their greatest power is their ability to obstruct legislation that is not in their interest. They have the congressional votes to stop any attempt at adopting a constitutional amendment. And the out-of-date words in the second part of Article V are a gift for their desire to obstruct. It is easy to stop people from doing something that has never been done before.

Billionaires, large corporations, politicians, and

special interest groups, with an ideology that supports greed and lust for power, all work together. An attack on one draws a powerful and calculated response by all. When a mass shooting occurred, within minutes the words 'thoughts and prayers' came from the mouth of every politician in that group. Practiced perfected responses fill the media for every critical issue. Think tanks stand ready to produce uniform instantaneous responses for their politicians and pundits. In recent years, the group has created a fortress. Domination of popular media, unlimited funding, and unified ideology provide support. But this group cannot claim moral authority.

The autocratic group is sympathetic to actions taken by dictators and lacks the guidance of laws, fairness, or civil responsibility. Rigging the system is an optional strategy. The Ayn Rand philosophy of self-determination overrides civil responsibility.

The ideology of our Founders embraced civil responsibility, accepted that we are all created equal, and set up a system of checks and balances to control the excesses of party-over-country actors. Will of the people and moral authority are the guardrails of our government.

Democracy is not a spectator sport. If we just sit around and watch, we are playing into the hands of those who do not care about preserving our representative democracy. The politics of inevitability leads us to accept that fate has ordained supply-side economics, a biased Supreme Court, and other government flaws.

But the many obstacles give us a reason to reinvent our thinking and pursue a rebirth of ideas. Our Founders could not predict and design a system for creating constitutional amendments that would be fully functional a dozen generations in the future. But they did give us the principles on which the system should be based.

The function of our representative democracy is based on the will of the people.

We see Article V as a reasonable, but not necessarily easy, path to amend the Constitution. Close inspection of the words in Article V is helpful. The document has the words, *"convention for proposing amendments."* It does not say whether the convention should have a few delegates or hundreds of delegates. It does not say that the convention cannot be online. It does not dictate what actions the delegates may or may not take. The only thing we know is that the *"convention"* must meet the legal definition of the word.

In 1787 it was not possible for regular communication between delegates at a convention and their constituents back in their home states. All systems of communication took days or weeks. It was necessary to send delegates to debate and draft legislation.

Today, communication can be instantaneous. The idea of sending a delegate to an Article V convention to debate and draft legislation, without vetting those actions in their home state, is a non-starter for most voters. This is a big part of the reason that the states have never held an Article V convention.

It is unreasonable to think that two-thirds of Congress, in this increasingly partisan time, would agree to any new constitutional amendment. Our Founders expected this possibility and built the second part of Article V into the Constitution as a remedy. In 1787, the best and brightest of their time concluded that a full-blown convention was the best solution for drafting amendments and continuing toward ratification of those amendments. These well-informed lawyers and community leaders used their collective personal knowledge to reach that conclusion.

Today, because of years of traditional interpretation, we accept the old idea that we must draft the words of new amendments to the Constitution behind closed doors if we choose a state-initiated Article V convention. That has never happened and may never happen.

If those same fifty-five delegates were alive today and had the common experiences of our time, including over two hundred years of American history, their conclusions may be drastically different. They may consider drafting an amendment behind closed doors to be foolhardy, ridiculous, and out of touch with today's norms. Hanging on to archaic procedure makes no sense. But the words that those men drafted do not change.

Our elected representatives, constitutional experts, and judges feel obligated to stick with the common interpretation of those words.

In his lecture 'The Path of the Law,' printed in the Harvard Law Review in 1898, Oliver Wendell Holmes made this oft-quoted observation: *"It is revolting to have no better reason for a rule of law than that it was so laid down in the time of Henry IV. It is still more revolting if the grounds upon which it was laid down have vanished long since and the rule simply persists from blind imitation of the past."*

In more recent decades, we have used the concept of a 'limited convention' in state applications for an Article V convention. These applications limit the topics of discussion to one topic. For example, the delegates may discuss term limits or balancing the budget.

In 1787, delegates got together with the intention of amending the Articles of Confederation. In effect, they were holding a 'limited convention.' But they expanded their actions and created a whole new constitution. Scholars fear that any convention called as a 'limited convention' could also expand their actions and propose amendments beyond the scope of what the states contemplated when they applied for the convention. It raises the specter of radical and unexpected change such as repeal of the Bill of Rights. Those expanded actions would result a 'runaway convention.'

We should not hold a constitutional convention based on a whim and a promise. The whim is a poorly defined issue. The promise is that the delegates will act responsibly.

Even though amendment ratification by thirty-eight states would still be necessary, any unplanned actions by the delegates would undermine the credibility of the entire process. The concept of a 'limited convention' has not ended fears of a 'runaway convention.' Concerned citizens fear that mischievous delegates will manipulate the rules.

In addition, it is a large undertaking to hold a national convention for one issue. Obtaining national support for a poorly defined concept is part of the problem. People may ask 'what is the limitation on terms?' or 'will a balanced budget involve a reduction in entitlement benefits?'

Another one of the drawbacks of having a full-blown Article V convention is that the procedures would not allow an extended period for vetting the proposals prior to the convention vote. The delegates at the convention would not wait for public approval of a newly drafted amendment while they sat around the convention hall. This feature of a full-blown Article V convention does not meet ordinary expectations of today's voters.

The intent of bypassing an intransigent Congress was a sincere effort to ensure that the will of the people would prevail. In the minds of the Founders, creating the possibility of an Article V convention fulfilled their aspirations. But our Founders' intentions are becoming lost in the modern-day political landscape.

Leaders of both political parties have each adopted a posture that blocks attempts to amend our Constitution. Republican Party leadership likes the status quo. Their supporters are reaping the benefits of favorable tax laws, biased judges, gerrymandering, and existing constitutional flaws that favor their interests. Their leaders oppose measures that could harm those engrained advantages.

The Democratic Party fears that if we drafted the amendment language behind closed doors, the people in this country could not properly express their opinions on the issue. A hall filled with delegates approved by state legislatures creates the possibility of power brokers and backroom deals. Currently, Republicans dominate more than half of state legislatures and Democrats fear that the process would give the Republicans the advantage. The Convention of States, a right-wing advocacy group, has made substantial progress toward an Article V convention. This group has proposed a balanced budget amendment. That could allow convention delegates, acting behind closed doors, to shape an ultra-conservative national budget. That scares the opposition and causes negative sentiment for holding the Article V convention.

Our elected representatives are shortchanging the American people. Greed, party politics, and misunderstanding are diminishing our rights. It is the right of the people to alter our government. That is part of our Declaration of Independence.

As we examine the need for altering our government, it would be hard to look past the lack of oversight of the Supreme Court. Thomas Jefferson wrote the Declaration of Independence. He also famously said: *"You seem to consider the judges as the ultimate arbiters of all constitutional questions; a very dangerous doctrine indeed, and one which would place us under the despotism of an oligarchy. Our judges are as honest as other men, and not more so."*

Some of today's new court rulings appear to represent a political agenda rather than an exercise in jurisprudence. *Citizens United* and *Dobbs* are prime examples of rulings that oppose the majority opinion of the voters.

Many political leaders have made a calculated decision to not engage in major reform efforts. They avoid voting on controversial issues like abortion and gun control. It is too easy to argue over the concept and blame the other side for the lack of action. That increases support from the party base and angers the other party. As the partisan divide widens, politicians do little or nothing for their state or the country. This explains the continuing low approval rating for Congress. The people want legislative solutions, not endless disagreement.

The intent of our Founders was to let the will of the people take the lead. We should consider their intent to outweigh the obstacles that occur due to the passage of time. This sentiment encourages us to reexamine the words in Article V.

Congress has become inflexible. Lobbyists for entrenched interests have imposed their will. By default, the opportunity and obligation to amend the Constitution falls to state legislators.

The opportunity for lobbyists to influence state legislators is tiny as compared to the opportunity to influence members of Congress. There are 535 members of Congress in one location while there are 7,386 state legislators scattered across fifty locations. Each state legislator has only about half as many days on the job. Members of the United States House of Representatives represent about 700,000 people. On average, each state legislator in a state House of Representatives represents only 45,000. It is far easier for the average voter to successfully contact their state legislator and it is more difficult for lobbyists.

State legislators are more likely to respond to the will of the people.

If we change our way of thinking and utilize the opportunity to work with state legislators on national reform issues, we can improve the chances of correcting the flaws in our government.

'Fully Restricted' Convention

We have adopted seventeen amendments since 1787. In each case, Congress, by a two-thirds majority of the House and the Senate, approved the amendments. But this amendment process has stalled.

In theory, we could use a national referendum to amend the Constitution. But that is direct democracy. Our Founders and many of today's scholars oppose creating national laws by popular vote. It is not part of our system of laws. It is not legal.

It is possible to have an 'open' convention. At this type of convention, delegates may discuss any topic. This was acceptable at the time of our Founders but is less acceptable today. Many have fears of a 'runaway convention' where the delegates could start the process of tearing apart constitutional norms and act in a way that the public does not want. Today, neither the people nor their elected state representatives want to give that kind of power to a set of delegates. This is the major reason that the states have never held an 'open' Article V convention.

Courts have examined and approved the possibility of holding a 'limited convention.' This type of convention would limit discussion to those issues listed on the state applications of thirty-four states. The concept of a 'limited convention' has not eliminated fears of a 'runaway convention.'

Yet the only legal way to bypass Congress is by using an Article V convention. We should eliminate the possibility of a 'runaway convention.' We could draft each amendment before the convention and not leave it up to the delegates. It must be possible to deal with more than one issue without the large-scale undertaking of a full-blown convention for each issue.

When we perceive that an Article V convention is a place where behind-the-scenes negotiations take place, we close the door in fear of the results of those negotiations. But when we understand the function of a 'fully restricted' Article V convention, the door swings wide open. Full transparency is critical. At this type of convention, nothing happens behind closed doors.

The concept of a 'limited convention' is not in the words of the Constitution. Nor is the concept of a 'fully restricted' convention. But neither option is prohibited. In fact, a 'fully restricted' convention may be a type of 'limited convention.' We need to pursue the amendment process with available tools.

George Washington said that it is the right of the people to amend the Constitution. He did not say that it is the right of party-over-country elected representatives to amend the Constitution.

He did not say that we should allow the biased intent of special interests to override our rights. The sentiment of the voters should drive the bus.

If we put the word 'convention' under the microscope we find that we have the choice to minimize the actual meeting and the function of that meeting. We may define a convention as a body set up by agreement to deal with a particular issue. There is no necessity for discussion, or power brokers, or back-room deals. The actual 'convention' could be just a procedural formality.

This possibility was supported by the United States Supreme Court in its 2020 ruling, *Chiafalo v Washington.* Elena Kagen stated that nothing in the Constitution prohibits states from removing the discretion of the delegates.

Thus far, Congress has taken the lead for all new amendments. This is the front end of a two-step procedure. The two legislative bodies in Congress have well-established procedural rules and meet on a regular basis in a well-established location. The back end of the process is ratification (approval) by three quarters of the states. Article V allows an alternative procedure to be the front end of the two-step procedure. Individual states may start the process.

Accepted procedure is that if two thirds of the states (thirty-four states) choose to get together and hold a 'convention,' they may agree on exact language and complete the front end of the process. The back end of the process, ratification by thirty-eight states, remains the same.

But the 'convention' process is not well-developed. This legislative body has no established procedural rules, no established meeting time, and no designated meeting place. We do not even know how many delegates should attend or what level of power they would have to act on behalf of their respective states.

A 'fully restricted' Article V convention redefines the front end of the two-step procedure. Thirty-four states would still need to agree on the language of the proposed amendment. But the process of reaching agreement would change. We may draft the language in advance and not at the 'convention.' The 'convention' would have little need for procedural rules because delegates would do no more than cast their states' vote for the established amendment language. The number of delegates would be mostly irrelevant. The time and place of the 'convention' would be simplistic and inexpensive as compared to a 'full blown' convention.

In addition to the *Chiafalo* ruling, history demonstrates that individual states have the authority to control the actions of their delegates at the convention. That precedent was set in 1787 when the New Hampshire delegation did not vote to approve the Constitution. After going back to the state leaders for approval, they changed their vote.

States can achieve state approval of a proposed amendment in any of three ways. Voters may create and vote on a ballot initiative in the states that allow this process. Or a state legislature may hold a referendum that allows the voters to approve the measure. Either of these provides a direct democracy influence. Alternatively, the state legislature may approve the measure without a separate vote by the people.

Proposed Amendments

A constitutional amendment is necessary to change

any language in the Constitution. Congress may create and change laws for other issues. The intended function of the Supreme Court is to interpret laws. Court rulings have the effect of laws, but the process should not change existing language written into the Constitution or change laws passed by Congress. This leaves gray areas where it is not obvious whether Congress or the Supreme Court has the authority. It was our Founders' intention that the people have the ultimate authority.

As we try to correct a government flaw, we also must try to figure out whether a new constitutional amendment is necessary. In some cases, like placing term limits on Supreme Court justices, the answer is clear. The language of the Constitution implies that they have no term limit. Any change requires a new amendment.

Placing term limits on members of Congress does not require a new amendment. But without a new amendment, it is foolhardy to think that this could happen. They have a disincentive to limit their own term of service. Therefore, a new amendment makes sense.

It is more difficult to make sense of the proper correction method for other flaws in government. Polls show that the people want to overturn the *Citizens United* Supreme Court ruling. That ruling overturned *Austin,* an earlier Supreme Court ruling, and prior legislation passed by Congress. It is possible that the Supreme Court could overturn its own ruling. It is not clear if Congress could pass a law overturning the *Citizens* ruling. Since neither is likely to occur soon, a new amendment makes the most sense.

Normally, Congress decides government health care policy. The Supreme Court has not been involved. Details of health care delivery are too complicated for a constitutional fix. But if the voters want to set up universal coverage without specific details of that coverage, and Congress does not comply, then a constitutional amendment may be the logical solution. More than half of the countries in the world have a form of health care guarantee written into their constitutions.

Gun rights present a problematic challenge. The Supreme Court has subjectively found that the Second Amendment to the Constitution gives Americans the right to bear arms for self-defense. Congress has avoided recent major legislation dealing with gun regulation. A new constitutional amendment may overturn the *Heller* decision or ban assault rifles. It is unclear whether this would affect the Second Amendment. It is unclear whether the federal government would be involved with other gun regulations; the states may enact related laws.

A notable majority of the people should favor any proposed amendment, not just a razor-thin majority. Government works best when it does not change for light and transient causes. This is why a national referendum, with the possibility of a small winning margin, is not in our best interest. An amendment supported by state legislative action or statewide votes, in the required number of states, would have a mandate, not just a razor thin margin.

The following amendments may improve our representative democracy. They are starting points for further discussion and debate.

Overturn Citizens United

A total of 803 local government resolutions calling for a constitutional amendment to overturn Citizens United have been passed since the 2010 Supreme Court Ruling. Nineteen states and Washington D.C. have called for a Constitutional amendment. Dozens of members of the 118th Congress have co-sponsored legislation to overturn Citizens United in the 'Democracy For All Amendment'.

Supreme Court Justice John Paul Stevens suggested an amendment having the following language *"Neither the First Amendment nor any other provisions of this Constitution shall be construed to prohibit the Congress or any state from imposing limits on the amount of money that candidates for public office, or their supporters, may spend in election campaigns."*

An amendment to the Constitution is necessary here to overturn the Supreme Court ruling.

Ban Gerrymandering

A state may have a ballot initiative, a referendum vote or direct legislature vote with the following language in its effort to ban gerrymandering:

"The state of Missouri (or another state) shall take those steps necessary to cast an Article V convention vote in favor of amending the United States Constitution with the following language and no other language; Whenever a state's redistricting map shows bias, that state shall correct the bias."

Abolish the Electoral College

This amendment becomes reasonable only after eliminating gerrymandering in all the states.

Suggested proposal language: *"The President shall be elected by receiving a plurality of votes from the most congressional districts; in addition, two votes are added for receiving a plurality of votes in a state; if no candidate receives more than half of the votes (formerly known as electoral votes), the tiebreaker shall be that the candidate with the most popular votes wins the election."*

A constitutional amendment may be necessary here to clarify election procedure.

Term Limits on Congress

Suggested proposal language: *"The term of members of the United States House of Representatives shall be limited to sixteen years and the term of members of the United States Senate shall be limited to twenty-four years."*

Other term limitations are possible.

Ranked-Choice Voting

Suggested language: *"A single nonpartisan blanket primary shall be used in federal elections and Ranked-Choice-Voting shall be used in the subsequent general election."*

Reproductive Rights Law

Suggested language: 1. *"Reproductive rights are inherent rights, natural rights, or common law rights; Article III of the Constitution does not give power to affirm or deny these rights to the United States Supreme Court. 2. Congress shall control reproductive rights decisions. If Congress fails to create reproductive rights law within two years from the date of ratification of this amendment, industry guidelines shall be the default position subject to congressional disapproval."*

Nine unelected, potentially partisan, judges cannot solve the abortion controversy. The hope of electing judges with similar abortion policy often sways elections. Congresspeople do not want to vote on abortion rights. But our Founders wanted our elected representatives to make decisions on precedent setting election-swaying issues, not the courts. Taking the Supreme Court out of the picture will reduce our partisan divide.

A congressional vote can resolve this issue. It is not well suited for an amendment to the Constitution. But Congress has refused to act on the issue. An amendment to the Constitution may be necessary here to set aside Supreme Court rulings.

Ban Assault Weapons

Suggested proposal language: "The State of California (or another state) shall take those steps necessary to cast its Article V convention vote in favor of amending the United States Constitution with the following language and no other language: "*1. The United States bans non-military sale and use of assault weapons and other weapons of war. 2. The right to bear arms for self-defense is an inherent right, a natural right, or common law right; Article III of the Constitution does not give power to affirm or deny this right to the United States Supreme Court*".

This amendment would overturn part of *Heller* and may not affect the Second Amendment.

Taking this 'hot button' issue out of the court system forces Congress to take on this lawmaking responsibility. It would also take away the incentive to appoint radical judges when the purpose of their appointment is to stake out minority positions on this issue. Absent national legislation on non-military weapons, gun regulation would fall to state legislatures.

An amendment to the Constitution is not mandatory here. But it may clarify our right to bear arms for self-defense. Any move to restrict gun use would send a message that gun safety is what the people want.

Adopt Universal Health Care

We may use the following language to adopt universal health care for the United States. The state of Michigan (or another state) shall take those steps necessary to cast its Article V convention vote in favor of amending the United States Constitution with the following language and no other language: *"Universal health care is an inalienable right; the United States Congress shall use due diligence to develop and initiate a system of universal health care for its citizens".*

Adopting this amendment would force Congress to create a system of health care comparable to all the other developed countries. It does not mandate which system to adopt. It only mandates that we provide health care service to everyone.

An amendment to the Constitution is not mandatory here. Congress could act at any time. But health care industry giants have blocked universal health care in the past and may continue to do so in the future. A move to amend the Constitution may be the only way to force action that follows the will of the people.

First Amendment Restrictions

Suggested proposal language: *"Under the First Amendment, freedom of speech rights granted to media outlets shall not include or enhance dissemination of falsehoods, which cause harm to citizens of the United*

States or threaten the function of our government."
Violations would occur when an informed person would conclude that:

- The statements were false.
- The statements could, directly or indirectly, cause death or harm.
- The statements were intentional propaganda.

This is different than the Fairness Doctrine. That controlled fairness in the media presentation of differing ideologies.

This is different that the Sedition Act of 1798. That act penalized those who merely criticized the government. Individuals or newspaper editors did the criticism. Organizations with national influence did not control those individuals.

The amendment is necessarily on a slippery slope. Harm to individuals and threat to our government are both subjective. But unrestricted freedom of speech rights by media organizations has led to undesirable and unethical consequences. The amendment will let the courts determine if the actions are harmful. This would cause media outlets to consider the risk of disseminating harmful propaganda. The most flagrant falsehoods and the most impactful media outlets may receive the most scrutiny.

This change requires an amendment to the Constitution.

Term Limits on the Supreme Court

Suggested language: *The President shall nominate a new Supreme Court justice in odd numbered years. The Senate may provide advice and consent for the nominee after the nomination. The President may replace the nominee if the Senate rejects the nominee but the power to nominate the new justices is not subject to Senate veto. The number of justices shall always be nine.*

The language here outlines the basic concept. Added language may be necessary to spell out what happens when an unexpected vacancy occurs.

Secret Impeachment Votes

Suggested language: *"All impeachment votes shall be secret."*

This rule change requires a constitutional amendment to override traditional legislative protocol.

SCOTUS Confirmation Reform

Suggested language: *"Confirmation of judges to the United States Supreme Court shall include approval by Senators that represent the majority of the population of the United States."*

An amendment to the Constitution is necessary here because it will override the Senate's ability to occasionally make partisan choices that lead to biased Supreme Court justices.

No Lame-Duck Pardons

Suggested language: *"A lame-duck President shall not issue any Presidential pardons after the presidential election and before the end of his or her term in office."*

This requires a constitutional amendment because it alters the pardon power of the President as spelled out in Constitution.

Fix Article V

Suggested language: *"The Constitution may be amended by approval of three-quarters of state legislatures; voter initiated advisory referendums shall be available in each state for each proposed amendment; the state legislatures shall cast a timely vote subsequent to the advisory referendum."*

Adding language to the Constitution requires a Constitutional amendment.

Role of State Legislators

We have at least eight issues where polls show that a large majority of people favor change. Issues such as gerrymandering, limiting terms on the United States Supreme Court, overturning *Citizens United*, and banning assault rifles have had major national attention. The country is ready for action. With an overly partisan Congress, the responsibility of correcting the flaws in our Constitution shifts to state legislators.

But the states have never held an Article V convention. State legislators are content with the United States Constitution. They are indifferent about taking charge of the amendment process because that has not been part of their job description. Candidates and political parties perceive that if no one is talking about an issue (at the state level) then they cannot win votes by taking a stand on that issue.

Since the last time that we proposed and ratified a new Constitutional amendment, the states have made 145 applications for an Article V convention. The top four issues were balanced budget and fiscal restraint (77), reproductive rights

(19), term limits on Congress (19), and campaign finance (5).

Here is an April 2023 application by the state of Oklahoma:

A Joint Resolution relating to a Constitutional Convention pursuant to Article V of the United States Constitution; application; distribution.

SUBJECT: Constitutional Convention

NOW, THEREFORE, BE IT RESOLVED BY THE HOUSE OF REPRESENTATIVES AND THE SENATE OF THE 1ST SESSION OF THE 59TH OKLAHOMA LEGISLATURE:

Section 1. The Oklahoma Legislature of Oklahoma hereby makes an application to Congress, as provided by Article V of the Constitution of the United States of America, to call a convention limited to proposing an amendment to the Constitution of the United States of America to set a limit on the number of terms that a person may be elected as a Member of the United States House of ENR. H. J. R. NO. 1032 Page 2 Representatives and to set a limit on the number of terms that a person may be elected as a Member of the United States Senate.

Section 2. The Secretary of State is hereby directed to transmit copies of this application to the President and Secretary of the Senate of the United States and to the Speaker, Clerk and Judiciary Committee Chairman of the House of Representatives of the Congress of the United States, and copies to the members of the said Senate and House of Representatives from this State; also to transmit copies hereof to the presiding officers of each of the legislative houses in the several States, requesting their cooperation.

Section 3. This application shall be considered as covering the same subject matter as the applications from other States to Congress to call a convention to set a limit on the number of terms that a person may be elected to the House of Representatives of the Congress of the United States and the Senate of the United States; and this application shall be aggregated with same for the purpose of attaining the two-thirds of states necessary to require Congress to call a limited convention on this subject, but shall not be aggregated with any other applications on any other subject. Section 4. This application constitutes a continuing application in accordance with Article V of the Constitution of the United States of America until the legislatures of at least two-thirds of the several states have made applications on the same subject.

The Oklahoma State Senate voted thirty-one to eleven in favor of this resolution that attempts to set term limits on Congress. That chamber has forty Republicans and eight Democrats. The sponsors were members of the Republican Party.

A closer look at the 145 applications shows that red state legislatures promoted red state issues and blue state legislatures promoted issues favored by blue states. Effectively, the applications were ideological statements saying hooray for our side. Media coverage of these applications has not caused national conversations.

Each of the fifty-five delegates who created our Constitution had something in common. They were well informed and did not belong to an organized political party. Special interest lobbyists were not around. Newspapers provided the only media influence. Public input and personal conscience dominated their agenda.

Today, media outlets do not subscribe to a fairness doctrine and typically promote a partisan message. Without any intent on our part, we have become indoctrinated into the thinking of 'our' party.

Our Founders added Article V to our Constitution for the purpose of updating our system of laws in a non-partisan manner. The best way for legislators to approach the concept of amending the Constitution is to assume perspective like those who drafted the Constitution. They must take off their partisan hats.

We see the tall tasks of informing voters, informing state legislators, eliminating fear of a runaway convention, overcoming partisan media, and having voters take the lead.

Action is necessary because we face a rising tide of distrust of government and political unrest. As Bob Dylan stated: *"We had better start swimming or we'll sink like a stone, for the times they are a changing."* If we take a complacent posture and fail to use critical thinking, our system of government may fail. Old systems often become less functional. If we avoid the state-initiated process of adding new amendments, we may sink into unsafe territory.

We see signs of recent threats to our form of government. Mitch McConnel failed to hold a confirmation hearing for the President's Supreme

Court nominee. We had an insurrection on January 6th, 2021. And Congress may have successfully removed the President from office in 2021 if we had secret impeachment votes. In recent years, political parties have increased the level of punishment for those who vote their conscience rather than the party interests. And dark money flows to party loyalists.

Times have changed since the 1960's and 1970's.

Instead of reacting to the will of the people, politicians have ignored the will of the people.

The Influence of Direct Democracy

Polls demonstrate our national desire to alter our government. The polarization that deters our opportunities for change occurs from the top down, from media and party loyalists. Dinner table discussions are not as polarized. Our innate tendencies to either get along or engage in conflict have not changed in the last few centuries.

All the amendments adopted since 1787 involved the use of Congress as the first step. We will call that Plan A. In each case, a bipartisan vote was necessary. That is unlikely today because of our increasing partisan divide.

The states have made attempts to amend the Constitution by holding a full-blown Article V convention. We will call that Plan B. Recent attempts have failed. Because we have never had an Article V convention, we do not have parameters of what the application process or the convention would be like.

Actions by the states have lacked bipartisan support. All new Constitutional amendments have obtained support from both parties. The concept of an Article V convention is poorly defined. The public cannot fully support a gathering with an unknown number of delegates and almost no convention rules. The reason for holding this Constitutional convention is not well-understood. The possibility of back-room deals and unscrupulous actors at the convention diminishes public support.

Plan B has no direct democracy influence. The opinion of the people sometimes differs from the party influenced votes of the state legislature. Recent statewide reproductive rights votes in Kansas and Ohio demonstrate this difference. Voters lack the ability to have effective influence on applications for an Article V convention when the measures have not been prewritten. For example, it is hard to contact your state legislators about term limits in Congress if the proposed length of the terms has not been determined.

Only state legislators have selected the issues on the applications. Concerned citizens may want other government reforms.

Direct democracy is where laws and policies imposed by governments are determined by the people themselves, rather than by representatives elected by the people. Neither Plan A nor Plan B include direct democracy influence.

In "Federalist No. 49", James Madison wrote: *"As the people are the only legitimate fountain of power, and it is from them that the constitutional charter, under which the several branches of government hold their power, is derived, it seems strictly consonant to the republican theory to recur to the same original authority ... whenever it may be necessary to enlarge, diminish, or new-model the powers of government."*

And when political parties take their marching orders from party bosses and special interests, legislators may thwart the will of the people. Bipartisan support may be present at the grass roots level but not by our elected representatives. For issues such as gun control, election reform, universal health care, and term limits on Congress, proposed legislation that reaches the desk of our elected representatives comes from a partisan source. And their vote on that legislation is mostly determined by the party's position. This results in built-in bias. With no direct democracy influence on the process of amending the Constitution, the process has become comatose, and our country may be busy dying.

Plan A and Plan B are not working. As a logical and prudent response, we can only look at what has not worked in the past and estimate what might work in the future. We need to develop Plan C. It should include bipartisan support and direct democracy influence.

With every political leader being projected as partisan and most media outlets having partisan leanings, we do not know if initiative-taking leadership and follow-up media attention would be successful.

History has shown that application for an Article V convention by a dozen or more biased state legislatures does not gain national attention.

But if a measure passed even one state legislature with bipartisan support, or even one statewide vote approved the measure in a bipartisan manner, it may gain attention. Momentum would be created if additional states voted and supported the measure. These actions are not part of Plan B even though state legislators are more accessible to the voters than members of Congress.

Unfortunately, state legislators may believe that only Congress has the power to introduce measures to amend the Constitution.

Plan C

The Constitution does not declare that states could introduce new, fully drafted, Constitutional amendments into their state legislatures as part of the state-initiated part of Article V. But it also does not prohibit that action. Legislatures elected by the voters make our laws, not potentially biased delegates at a convention.

As a nation, we should not sit on the sidelines and continue to be complacent about fixing the flaws in our government. We should seek the path with the greatest chance of success by using the opinions of the people as the guiding force. The process must involve a national conversation. Plan A is dormant. Plan B is dysfunctional. We have a disoriented national mindset. Disinformation is rampant. We can define the problems and grasp public sentiment toward fixing those problems, but we lack national conversation and a tried-and-true method of solving those problems.

It is not about what the delegates at the convention want; it is about what the people in their state want. Sinister actors may influence or control the delegates. It is far more difficult to control the opinions of the people of an entire state. Restricting the function of the delegates makes sense in this era of well-funded partisan players. The voters elected legislators to draft and vote on legislative measures. The voters did not elect them to send delegates to do that job.

There is no silver bullet. Plan C is a set of possibilities. It does not involve change in law, just a new perspective on existing law. James Madison used examples in state government constitutions for reference and drafted the Bill of Rights on his own. Numerous opportunities exist for drafting legislation. Amendment language does not need to be drafted by Congress or by those attending an Article V convention.

State legislators have the power to initiate and ratify amendments to the Constitution without the votes of Congress or approval by the President. Effectively, it is one large legislative body. This legislative body has the power to act without sending untrustworthy delegates to a convention. (We must follow the words in Article V; therefore, we must hold a symbolic convention.) There is no need for convention rules. The state legislators already have rules, and each has a meeting place. There is no need to grapple with vague notions like fiscal responsibility or (undefined) term limits. This large legislative body must follow the path to enacting legislation that is clearly stated in Article V.

National discussion is a major part of the process. It favors democracy. Autocrats want to smokescreen the issues. If they challenge a procedure in court, they risk elevating the process into the national discussion. Democracy may be fragile. But the position of the autocrats may also be fragile when their undemocratic standards become exposed in a national discussion. Complacency favors a slide toward autocracy. National exposure favors the position with the moral high ground.

If we wish to diminish autocratic influences, for the purpose of preserving or representative democracy, direct democracy influence may be necessary. It empowers citizens to overcome sentiments of party-over-country legislators and breaks through the institutionalized barriers to accountability that arise in representative systems.

Without a degree of direct democracy, we must depend on leadership that claims to have a monopoly on reason. If this type of leadership is unchecked, we can look forward to a government dominated by competitive authoritarianism where greed and lust for power dominate the leadership agenda.

The influence of direct democracy is not available with Plan A or Plan B. Plan C allows a much greater opportunity for input of public sentiment. There are fourteen times as many state legislators as members of Congress. Concerned citizens and advocacy groups have a greater opportunity to convince a state legislator to introduce a measure into their respective legislature or pursue ballot initiatives.

Advocacy Groups

As a result of widespread sentiment that the people do not have adequate influence on our government, advocacy groups have become commonplace. They have product knowledge. They can work on writing and vetting new amendments and increase public awareness by using their extensive databases.

Major advocacy groups that would like to correct flaws in our Constitution include Common Cause, The League of Women Voters, Indivisible, Ballot Initiative Strategy Center, United States Term Limits, Unite America, Everytown for Gun Safety, and Move to Amend.

Conservative groups such as the Heritage Foundation and the Federalist Society show little interest in amending the Constitution. They advocate traditional values but are more likely to support competitive authoritarianism, a step down on the Democracy Index.

Currently, those seeking to amend the Constitution are pursuing Plan A or Plan B. They are not asking state legislators to draft proposals first and then proceed to an Article V convention.

Groups advocating proposals on the same issue could work together to write an amendment and seek state legislative support for it. For example, gun safety groups could work together to ban assault rifles. Groups such as Everytown for Gun Safety, Moms Demand Action for Gun Safety in America, The Brady Campaign, Americans for Responsible Solutions, Law Center to Prevent Gun Violence, and Coalition to Stop Gun Violence each have product knowledge.

But advocacy groups may not fully understand available opportunities. Their passion for reform may not be fully tempered with deliberate reasoning and recognition of the obstacles. We need to use all available tools and not just rely on outdated tools. It is time to bypass party-over-country legislators and go directly to the people, just as our Founders suggested. Reform legislation in Congress, often started or supported by advocacy groups, may do no more than make a political statement intended to gain support from their base.

Each advocacy group should seek bipartisan co-sponsors to introduce state legislation to amend the United States Constitution. A call to action by that advocacy group would increase support for the proposed amendment. This would encourage legislative action in other states for the same measure.

Carpe Diem (Seize the Day)

Timid perspective and acceptance of normalized efforts to reform our government may accomplish little or nothing.

Draft the proposal. Send it to your state legislators. If an advocacy group sent out a call to action and its supporters subsequently sent out the proposal to many state legislators, the effect would be enhanced. And if many advocacy groups sent out many proposals on many issues, the chances of gaining national attention would be vastly improved. Drafted legislation gets attention.

The Agenda of a State Legislator

Party loyalty and party influence dominate their agendas in this partisan era.

Special interest groups promote an agenda or an ideology but not necessarily the best interest of the country. Their interests affect the positions taken by the political parties.

The profit-motivated media, in general, has a polarizing effect on Congress and our state legislatures. But it can be fickle. It enhances existing spoon-fed party positions but also enhances any political momentum. Public input can have a strong impact. It would be much easier to get a proposed Constitutional amendment onto the agenda of a state legislator than getting it onto the agenda of a member of Congress. But that has not happened. Tradition, perception, and complacency have been in the way.

State Ballot Initiatives/Referendums

The initiative or referendum process is a momentum builder. It brings the topic and specific wording into the national conversation. It instigates robust debate that is necessary to properly address issues of national concern.

Bipartisan effort is necessary for success. Votes are the most accurate and bipartisan indication of public sentiment.

The 2022 Kansas referendum vote to not ban abortions shocked the political world. The state legislature wanted to ban abortions. They picked a date on the calendar when the legislature expected low voter turnout. The high voter turnout and unexpected result clearly showed that the legislators were not acting on behalf of the will of the voters. The vote reflected conscience, not party loyalty.

If we extrapolate the Kansas vote, using voting trends from prior elections, we can estimate that forty-five states would favor the reproductive rights issue that passed in Kansas.

In 2018, Michigan, because of a ballot initiative, voted sixty-one percent to thirty-nine percent to ban gerrymandering. Extrapolating that vote indicates that thirty-seven states would support that ban.

A ballot initiative occurs by obtaining enough signatures on petitions. About half of the states allow this method of initiating a statewide vote. In these states, the voters have that opportunity even if their state legislators do not want that issue on the ballot. Voter turnout in states with an initiative or referendum on the ballot is three to eight percent higher than in states without an initiative or referendum on the ballot.

Statewide votes get attention. Big money and political party interests have less influence on voters than on their elected representatives. Polls, pundits, and politician's rhetoric are at best ineffective and at worst a smokescreen to avoid taking meaningful action. Corporations, the wealthy, and special interests have less opportunity to influence the outcome when we have a public vote. It is much harder to throw shade on a firm proposal. Back-room deals cannot happen if the measure is already complete.

A statewide vote by ballot initiative or referendum shows the margin of favorability to the whole country. It is a wake-up call for Americans who have not been paying attention to the issue.

Representative democracy should protect the interests of the underrepresented. But it is foolhardy to believe that the interests of greed and lust for power are underrepresented at any level of today's government. They fear the influence of direct democracy and the will of the people. It is not surprising that this group is making an earnest effort to get rid of the state ballot initiative opportunity. This is the front line of the battle between opposing ideologies.

Implementation of Plan C

We have several potential courses of action but no established path. In addition to informing voters and state legislators, we need to avoid the pitfalls of overly partisan applications while having voters take the lead.

Co-sponsors of legislation from each political party would send a bipartisan message and set the table for success.

We may choose the break-the-ice approach and select a proposed amendment that has the best chance of approval by thirty-eight states. A new amendment would increase civic awareness and may lead to national discussion of other amendments. Limiting Congressional terms and overturning *Citizens United* have the highest polling favorability.

State legislators may choose to introduce Constitutional amendment language on the hot topics such as reproductive rights and gun rights. If referendums were held, the results would show the level of support by each political party in that state. Extrapolation of these voting results would help us to estimate the number of states that might support the measure.

Influential advocacy groups may choose to promote issues where they have the product knowledge. Country First or League of Women's Voters could try to end gerrymandering.

A motivated state legislature may send a

message to the rest of the country by approving an amendment. If some members of the minority party voted with the majority, other states may follow. Would Connecticut vote to ban assault rifles?

Or we may choose an issue that we believe would have the highest impact on our representative democracy. Ranked Choice voting may reduce partisanship. Amending Article V would make it easier to amend the Constitution.

Leadership is a wild card in this process. A pragmatic leader on the state or federal level could move the process forward. Their credibility with both political parties would be critical. Spearheading a ballot initiative on a key issue, such as amending Article V, could jumpstart the entire process.

Several topics could be promoted at once. If advocacy groups worked together to promote a reform package, the overall impact would be greater. National media attention would be more likely. Introduction of numerous proposals into a state legislature would increase legislator's response. The feedback would tell us which topics are most likely to become part of the Constitution.

We may consider a package of four new Constitutional amendments that are most likely to reduce the partisanship that is threatening our representative democracy. Overturning *Citizens United* would reduce the interest of corporations and their right-wing bias. Ending gerrymandering would change the makeup of Congress and could reduce lawmakers bias toward party rather than the interests of the country. Ranked choice voting would reduce the number of radical politicians in our legislatures. First Amendment restrictions would reduce scorched-earth rhetoric in public media.

More issues in the conversation will sharpen the debate. Debate on factual differences of opinion between candidates may replace discussion of weakly defined issues of passion. These discussions may influence state legislative elections and elections of members of the United States Congress. It is not about being Republican or Democrat. Both conservatives and progressives may support those issues that would improve our government.

A 'limited convention,' by rule, restricts the number of Article V convention issues. An 'open' convention was the basic design of our Founders. It could deal with an unlimited number of issues. The concept of a 'fully restricted' convention is more in line with the design of our Founders. More than one ballot initiative or more than one referendum may appear on a statewide ballot. State legislatures may send more than one amendment to a 'fully restricted' Article V convention. Of course, the 'Fix Article V' amendment would eliminate the need for an Article V convention.

Just like other legislative measures, the process of amending the United States Constitution can begin with one legislator introducing a measure into the appropriate legislative body. With majority support from enough states, the measure becomes law.

In the United States Congress, measures can move quickly through the House and the Senate. With legislatures located in fifty states, the amendment approval process will move more slowly. That is a good thing as opposed to the time restraints that would occur with full-blown Article V convention. The additional time will give the public an opportunity to fully vet the issue. Statewide ballot initiatives and referendums may occur. A ballot initiative could show public opinion in a state where the people support the measure, but the elected representatives do not. When one informed state legislator starts the process, it would not be necessary to be overly concerned about the exact language of the proposal. The added time will allow for language revisions.

A state legislator may want to achieve personal recognition by being the first to promote a new amendment to the Constitution. Every candidate for state legislative office may post an online list of his or her favorite proposed amendments to the United States Constitution. And they can promote these issues as part of their campaign for office.

After establishing bipartisan support for a measure, all advocates can feel justified in lobbying state legislators from both political parties.

Voters will not need to know the technical details of a 'fully restricted' Article V convention. They just need to understand the words of the proposal and know that they are trying to amend the Constitution.

After the vetting process is completed, the state legislature can vote to send the proposed amendment to a 'fully restricted' Article V convention.

Nothing will happen behind closed doors. If the applications have differing language, the measure will go back to the individual states for approval of the new language. Coordination between the states, prior to the 'fully restricted' Article V convention, is important. Assistance from a national organization would be helpful.

The National Conference of State Legislators states that every state legislator and staffer is a member of the organization, and they have complete access to the latest in bipartisan policy research, training resources and technical assistance. But most of their sponsors are corporations. NCSL does not promote or coordinate efforts to amend the Constitution by use of the state-initiated part of Article V. Their corporate sponsors might leave if the group cooperated with efforts to pass new amendments that could hurt corporate profits.

The Council of State Governments does not have the subject of amending the Constitution on its agendas. The group is funded by the states and may be non-partisan, but it has not officially acknowledged the existence of the Constitution's reference to an Article V convention.

Creating a public website for proposing amendments to the Constitution would increase public awareness on national issues. State legislators could post proposed amendments and comments.

The public would have read-only access and might choose to make comments to their own state legislators. All 7,386 state legislators could make comments for or against any proposal or propose changes to the measure. The website could include a link to basic information about the process of amending the United States Constitution, including the ability of state legislators to propose amendments.

By commenting to their state legislators on measures shown on the site, all Americans, including young Americans, would have more influence on important national issues.

Legal Challenges

In recent years, brinksmanship has too often dominated our news cycle. Congressional approval ratings are at dismally low levels. Approval ratings for the Supreme Court and recent Presidents have declined. Indirectly, this is evidence that our government is flawed. Our Founders added Article V to the Constitution so that we the people could correct those flaws and create a more perfect union. If we fail to correct Constitutional flaws, our government may be in the grips of a terminal illness.

If an ideology that includes obstruction of efforts to reform our government maintains control, we the people will fail to achieve the aspirational goals of our Founders. And we will see a continued decline in the Democracy Index. A favorite tool of obstructionist ideology is flimsy legal challenges. We must be aware that some of the issues involve overturning Supreme Court rulings. Recently, the court has not been shy about ignoring potential conflict of interest. Obstructionists may challenge any definition of an Article V convention. At the state level, they may try to block the state votes for applications to an Article V convention.

The seldom used Ninth Amendment is relevant here. It states: *"The enumeration in the Constitution, of certain rights, shall not be construed to deny or disparage others retained by the people."*

The moral high ground gives the people the right to amend the Constitution. The Constitution also gives the states the right to choose that state's election procedures under the Tenth Amendment. Most states allow voters to exercise state rights to amend the state's constitution by referendum. But if those same states do not allow those same voters to exercise their federal rights to amend the United States Constitution, by referendum, then those states may be denying or disparaging the rights of those voters. The Ninth Amendment asserts that a natural right, such as the right to try to alter our Constitution, may be judicially enforceable unless there is specific and explicit positive law to the contrary.

Each state legislator has taken an oath to support the Constitution of the United States. If a state allows a vote on a state constitutional issue, it is logical that their oath would encourage a vote on a national constitutional issue.

At the federal level, Congress may try to obstruct the process. Article V states that *"Congress shall call a convention for proposing amendments."* We must not forget that 145 members of the House of Representatives voted against the routine certification of votes for President on January 6th, 2021. That same group may attempt to find a weak legal excuse to avoid calling an Article V convention. The intention of our Founders was to let the states bypass an uncooperative Congress. They did not want to give Congress the opportunity to obstruct efforts to bypass their own intransigence.

A large majority of the people favor change on issues such as banning assault rifles, getting rid of dark money, ending gerrymandering, and term limits on Congress. The Founders intended that 'consent of the governed' would dominate consent of our elected legislators. In George Washington's Farewell Address, he (with the help of Madison and Hamilton) said that correction of the wrongs in our government should reflect the 'opinion of the people.' He did not say that party-loyalists should have their way.

National attention matters. Misinformation and confusion are favorite tools of those who prefer competitive autocracy. But as positive momentum builds, media attention increases. Statewide votes thwart effort to throw shade on the moral high ground. Dinner table discussions result in swayed votes. National momentum may overcome weak obstructionist arguments made by those who oppose this democratic process.

If either state legislators or their legal advisors are concerned about obstruction of the Article V convention by Congress, they may choose the Fix Article V amendment as their first option. Once we have adopted that amendment, there will be few opportunities for legal challenges. Neither Congress, the President, nor the Supreme Court would have any part of this states' managed procedure. The amendment is a frontal challenge to those who prefer to never amend the Constitution.

Having a large-scale debate over the 'Fix Article V' amendment would be a positive development because it would increase civic awareness. The greater the controversy, the better the chance that we would adopt the amendment. The people and the states would hold moral high ground.

Summary

Our biggest problems may be complacency, apathy, and the perception of inevitability. We are content with our situation. We are not concerned about government flaws. We have resigned ourselves to our fate. Out of sight, out of mind. If no one else is talking about government reform, then we conclude that it is not important.

But that is a perfect recipe for those who wish to take advantage of our lack of interest. We dangerously assume that someone else is looking out for us. It is not the profit-motive media. It is not the party-over-county politicians, and it is certainly not big corporations.

We are on a slow journey leading to autocracy and we are not sure who is driving the bus. Serious issues have developed since the introduction and adoption of our last Constitutional amendment in 1971.

The opinions of those in corporate boardrooms, whose moral compass is guided by greed, often outweigh the desires of average Americans, and diminish the quiet enjoyment of the fruits of our labors.

Propaganda that rivals that in totalitarian countries is contaminating our public media. The falsehoods have accentuated our partisan divide. This ever-increasing divide threatens our form of government.

Our elections are not as free and fair as they once were.

Judges representing a minority party now dominate the Supreme Court and are more representative of party doctrine than jurisprudence and the will of the people.

Our laws allow us to worship the right to have an unheard-of level of gun violence.

Our health care system is second best to other comparable countries.

We can describe good government as full compliance with the words in our Constitution and the aspirations of our Founders. We call it a representative democracy or a democratic republic.

If we wish to keep our form of government, then we must understand the inherent threats to it and counter those threats. Most Americans believe that we should follow the aspirations of our Founders, the guardrails of our prior generations, or the common experience of other developed countries. The trend toward favoring the wealthy, corporations, and those who would prefer a more autocratic government has been increasing for decades. If we wish to end and reverse this trend, we must change the rules. Amending the Constitution is our most powerful opportunity.

Article V is not working. Congress is currently too partisan. And we certainly do not trust potentially biased delegates at a convention. But we have a third option. The 7,386 state legislators can function as a legislative body. That is cumbersome but has two advantages. It is easier for concerned citizens to contact their state legislators as compared to their United States congressperson. Secondly, we can insert a degree of direct democracy into the process. Recent votes in Kansas and Ohio show that voters can sometimes prevail over a party-over-country state legislature.

Statewide votes are more influential than pundits and polls. The battle for ballot initiatives is telling. Our country should welcome a full-blown battle over ballot initiatives. Autocratic wannabes would be fully exposed and would have nowhere to hide.

The most consequential thing that we could do to strengthen our representative democracy would be to overturn one or more Supreme Court rulings. Our government has done this several times in the past. We should not treat those judges as deities, they are just unelected citizens. That is an important check and balance that is currently missing.

Adopting a bundle of four amendments would decrease our partisan divide. Overturning *Citizens United*, ending gerrymandering, using ranked-choice-voting, and adding First Amendment restrictions would reduce the influence of those driven by greed and lust for power.

141

Introducing amendments to the United States Constitution into state legislatures would be more effective and have fewer legal challenges after adopting the 'Fix Article V' amendment.

We can improve the amendment process by convincing informed citizens to go directly to state legislators.

Carpe diem – seize the day. Politics is not a spectator sport.

Challenges to this new process for amending our Constitution will be based on fabricated legal technicalities. But the momentum of public sentiment can overcome the hurdles.

The path toward amending the Constitution will inspire robust debate. While this debate is occurring, whether it be at the dinner table, on television, at a town hall meeting, in a local tavern, or on a website forum, we are busy being born.

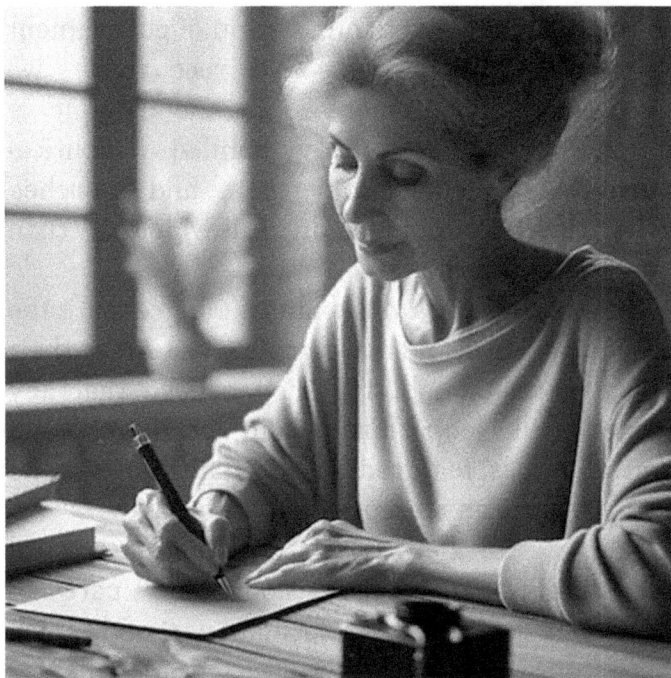

Addendum
Our Civic Responsibility

Back in 1775, average citizens risked their lives to fight for the chance to have a better government. During the Civil War, citizens risked their lives to fight for their preferred government. Many of our parents and grandparents fought in World War II. Today, we all have busy lives, and often feel that we are too busy to get involved in protecting our government. We collectively say: 'that is someone else's responsibility.'

Today's challenge to our system of government is from within our borders. Over recent years we have seen a steady increase in the amount of political violence, heavy-handed political maneuvering, media propaganda, and scorched earth rhetoric. Our political divide is wider now than at any time since the Civil War.

Members of the United States Congress are too busy campaigning and marching to the tune of their respective political party. They believe that any changes will jeopardize their privileges and rewards. Issues featured in the daily news cycle quickly replace any discussion of reform.

Members of state legislatures have a general understanding that they could be part of government reforms. It is a dormant part of their job description. They have not reacted to calls for change for two reasons. They expect Congress to act because Congress has acted in the past. And they are afraid to talk about issues that are not spoon fed to them by the media and their political party because they fear negative consequences, losing votes from stepping out of line.

Media outlets are pawns of the interests of their owners. It is all about profits. If government reform ideas do not sell advertisements, those reform ideas will not make the news.

The opportunity or responsibility falls to average citizens. Citizens organizations exist but have failed to gain enough momentum necessary to cause government change. They lack a direct conduit to the legislators that have the power.

Drafting the constitutional amendments in advance increases citizens power because it focuses on actionable measures rather than general ideas.

New constitutional amendments are not on the radar screen for state legislators, and average citizens are out of the loop. They are uninformed. And they are complacent. The status quo is too easy.

That makes wannabe autocrats happy. Conspiracy theories spread easily when average citizens do not bother to check the facts. Tell a lie three times and it becomes fact – Ayn Rand. And our Democracy Index ratings continue to decline as the partisan divide steadily increases. Complacency is the devil's workshop.

Citizen involvement can counter that trend. Those that refuse to seize opportunities to get involved are part of the problem. Not everyone will understand how to take steps to amend the Constitution and save our representative democracy, but those who have the opportunity have a moral and common-sense obligation. Our ancestors did not fail to get involved. If we sit on the sidelines, we will lose some of our freedoms. Future elections may be cancelled. Government troops may end peaceful demonstrations. Bribery may increase. Guilt or innocence of a defendant may depend on party loyalty. An autocratic government may ban books opposing their ideology. Party loyalty may be a litmus test for obtaining public employment positions like teachers, police officers, or government workers.

Democracy is fragile. When complacent citizens have the opportunity but do not get involved, we should question their reasoning. Their inaction may be the best interests of the enemies of representative democracy.

The conversation or debate over government reforms is the antidote to the poisons spread by overly biased media and by radical actors. Those conversations or debates put prominent issues on the table for those who have the power to make changes.

Plan of Action

Direct citizen conversation with members of the United States Congress is impractical because there are too many constituents for each member. And Congress is dysfunctional because of its large political divide. It has no opportunity to reach agreement on government reform issues.

State legislators are far more responsive to citizen inquiries. Writing letters to our state representatives is the simplified answer to our perplexing problem. To be most effective, the letters need to have specific components. Letters asking them to amend the United States Constitution will have the greatest impact.

Each letter should have basic components. You may need to explain why you are sending the letter to a state legislator instead of a member of the United States Congress. Here is some suggested wording: *Because of the large partisan divide in Congress today, and the need for amendments to the United States Constitution after more than fifty years of inactivity, the opportunity or obligation falls to state legislators.*

You should state your reasons for recommending the new amendment. Describe your passion and reasoning for improving our Constitution. For example, if you are recommending an eighteen-year term limit for Supreme Court justices, you might say:

We are the only country on earth that gives lifetime tenure to Supreme Court justices. About two-thirds of Americans want term limits. The nomination process has become overly controversial. Both conservatives and progressives agree that the term limit could be eighteen years.

Proposing a fully drafted amendment gives the state representative a specific proposal, not just a general idea. That makes it easier for the state representative to give an indication of approval or disapproval without hedging. It also appears professional and provides a framework for the proposed legislative action.

The state legislator understands that the boilerplate (legalese words that make it functional) and the proposed legislative language are only suggested words. It is the task of legislators to refine the language. You may start the letter with the words: *I ask for your consideration of the following proposal.*

The suggested boilerplate language may start out with:

A joint resolution applying to the Congress of the United States to call a convention to propose amendments to the Constitution of the United States.

Whereas it is the solemn duty of the states to protect the liberty of the people, particularly for generations to come, by proposing amendments to the Constitution of the United States through a convention of the states under Article V.

Be it therefore resolved by the legislature of the state of Michigan (or your state):

The legislature of the state of Michigan (or your state) herby applies to Congress, under the provisions of Article V of the Constitution of the United States, for the calling of a convention of the states for proposing an amendment to the Constitution of the United States with these words:

The President shall nominate a new Supreme Court justice in odd numbered years. The Senate may provide advice and consent for the nominee after the nomination. The President may replace the nominee if the Senate rejects the nominee but the power to nominate the new justices is not subject to Senate veto. The number of justices shall always be nine.

It is critical that, when a state applies for an Article V convention, the application addresses the voting power of the delegates at that convention. States have no reason to cede some of their negotiating power to convention delegates. The state can retain all its power by adding specific delegate restrictions to the application for the Article V convention such as:

Michigan (or your state) delegates to the Article V convention shall not vote on amendments to this proposal or vote on other proposed Constitutional amendments.

The remainder of the boilerplate language continues next:

The secretary of state is hereby directed to transmit copies of this application to the President and the Secretary of the United States Senate and to the Speaker and Clerk of the House of Representatives from this state; also transmit copies hereof to the presiding officers of each of the legislative houses in the several states, requesting their cooperation.

This application constitutes a continuing application in accordance with Article V of the Constitution of the United States until the legislatures of at least two-thirds of the several states made applications on the same subject.

Note that compiling the *italicized* words above creates a complete letter that you may send to your state representatives.

If you want to address a different issue, such as overturning the *Citizens United* ruling, you will substitute alternate phrasing into the above letter. The reasoning for recommending a new amendment may include comments such as:

Dark money creates too much political influence for corporations and rich Americans. This disenfranchises

149

other Americans. Those that supply financial support heavily influence too many of our elected representatives. They have each become puppets on a string with the biggest donors pulling the strings. A 2018 poll by the Center for Public Integrity found that three-fourths of Americans back a constitutional amendment outlawing Citizens United.

And proposed amendment language may read:

Neither the First Amendment nor any other provisions of this Constitution shall be construed to prohibit the Congress or any state from imposing limits on the amount of money that candidates for public office, or their supporters, may spend in election campaigns.

Sending a letter via the postal service has a greater impact than a letter sent electronically.

For those who are enthusiastic about one or more issues, a phone call to the legislative office may be more effective than a letter. The conversation may include the possibility of a state-wide referendum. A phone call and a letter would have an even greater impact. Of course, an in-person meeting would be best. Expect a businesslike conversation and keep in mind that the legislator may have a busy schedule.

Sharing the results of your efforts with others will allow coordination of everyone's efforts and increase the chances of achieving your objective. Coordinating efforts with advocacy groups is likely to increase the impact on state legislators.

- Some of the groups wishing to overturn *Citizens United* are American Promise, Common Cause, End Citizens United Action Fund, the NAACP, Public Citizen, U.S. PIRG, and Wolf-PAC.
- Groups that want to ban gerrymandering include Brennan Center for Justice, Campaign Legal Center, Common Cause, FairVote, League of Women Voters, and Public Mapping Project
- The Brennan Center for Justice supports term limits on Supreme Court justices.
- Groups seeking to overturn the *Dobbs* ruling include the American Civil Liberties Union, Center for Reproductive Rights, and Planned Parenthood.
- Ranked Choice Voting is supported by Unite America, FairVote, and Country First.

Each contact with a state legislator is incremental progress. Concerned citizen input will convince our state legislators to act on behalf of the prevalent opinion of their constituency. Citizen influence can be more powerful than party influence, lobbyist influence, or media dogma. When a state applies for an Article V convention for an issue such as term limits on Supreme Court justices, it will make national news and start a national conversation. Other states will consider the measure.

History has shown that bi-partisan support is necessary to adopt a new amendment to the United States Constitution. You may consider adding a phrase that encourages responsible action:

The best available evidence indicates that a majority of your constituents favor this measure. Moving forward provides an opportunity to set aside partisan bickering and pass meaningful bi-partisan legislation.

Getting involved in civics discussion is not for everyone. But the message can be effective. When concerned citizens contact their representatives with a clear and credible message, they are speaking for all those who favor the proposed amendment but choose not to get involved.

For more information go to the Concerned Citizens website at https://articlev.info/.

About The Author

Dale Leitzke is a lifelong observer of politics, human nature, voting patterns, political party dogma, and media fairness or bias. As a designated real estate appraiser, the prestigious Appraisal Journal published one of Dale's articles. As an appraiser he honed his ability to consider a wide range of divergent factors and draw a logical conclusion. In retirement, he continued his quest for knowledge by taking courses on the Constitution and the Supreme Court from Hillsdale college. His intense studies included careful examination of the writings and intent of our Founding Fathers. Critical thinking, scientific analysis, and deliberate reasoning drive his pursuit of government reforms.